REVANCHES

REVANCHES

Constellations, typestracts & other visual texts

1969-2009

Steve McCaffery

2015

Xexoxial Editions

West Lima, Wisconsin

Copyright © Steve McCaffery 2015

ISBN-10: 1-936687-25-9
ISBN-13: 978-1-936687-25-1

published by

Xexoxial Editions
10375 County Hway Alphabet
La Farge, WI 54639

www.xexoxial.org
perspicacity@xexoxial.org

Preface

Perhaps these poems were written for the brains of fleas, at least not the mind / brain opposition which lies at the basis of Cartesian theology. An insect world of insect works? Kafka would have relished this thought among the Hapsburg decomposition that gave birth to both himself and Freud. The lyric of rot might also work in places—a little too Bataille perhaps, and then again the deformation of signs is itself a master sign of Modernism. That said, domestic discourse networks emerge from pertinent, ambient technologies: ink and stylus, the first after petroglyphs, then that portable printing press the typewriter and the duplication machine, both ripe for creative misuse. The general title provides the French connection Revanches: revenge but in another related sense a recovery or retrieval, watkuweis in the Nez Perce language: a retrieval from being lost. The majority, if not all, texts in this book are previously unpublished and are retrieved from file folders in an archive.

CONSTELLATIONS	9
TYPESTRACTS	27
LETRASET POEMS	38
ORIGINS OF PROSE	42
2 SOUND POEMS	56
3 SEMIOTIC POEMS	59
MOON	63
RUBBER STAMP POEMS	67
ON A THEORY OF MAYA	83
MISCELLANEOUS HOLOGRAPHS	92
VISUAL COLLAGES	100
AGAINST WRITING	107
SIX VISUAL TEXTS	116
Notes of Composition	124

CONSTELLATIONS (1969-71)

```
                        ₁pharphar₁
                      ₁arpharpharphaɪ
                 ₁ɪarpharpharpharpharpharpharpharpharp₁
              ₁rpharpharpharpharpharpharpharpharpharphar
              ₁pharpharpharpharpharpharpharpharpharpharpɪ
              ₁rpharpharpharpharpharpharpharpharpharpharph
              ₁pharpharpharpharpharpharpharpharpharpharpha
              ₁pharpharpharpharpharpharpharpharpharpharphɑ
              arpharpharpharpharpharpharpharpharpharphar
              ₁rpharpharpharpharpharpharpharpharpharpha
              rpharpharpharpharpharpharpharpharph
              ₁rpharpharpharpharpharpharpharphar
              arpharpharpharphar harpharpharpharpharph
              ₁rpharpharpharpharpharpharpharphar
              rpharpharpharpharpharpharphₐ
              ₁pharpharpharpharpharpharphar
              arpharpharpharpharpyharpharphₐ
              rpharpharpharpharphar
              ₁pharpharpharpharph₆
              rpharpharpharph₆
              ₁pharpharphar₆
              rpharpharphar
              ₁rpharpharpʰ
              ₁rpharpʰ
```

```
                        s
                    s   m
                  s   m   i
                s   m   i   l
              s   m   i   l   e
            s   m   i   l   e   s
          s
        s
      s
                                          s
    s                                       s
      s                                   s
        s                               s
            s                       s
```

```
         e
        le
       tle
      ttle
     ittle
    little
     ittle
      ttle
       tle
        le
         e
        le
       ple
      pple
     ipple
    nipple
     ipple
      pple
       ple
        le
         e
```

```
                        ge           ist

                        ge           ist


        ta              ge


                        e            is


                                     ist
```

```
n e ! v e r

n e ? v e r

n e ( v e r

n e ) v e r

n e , v e r

n e : v e r

n e " v e r

n e - v e r

n e ; v e r

n e ' v e r

n e .
```

homage to jules verne

```
          s
        n o i r
          i
      m i r o i r
        i
        r
        a
        g
        e t o i l e
              l
              l
              u
              m a i s o n
l u m i e r e
```

```
T  REE
T  REE
THREE
   ARBOUR
 HARBOUR
 HARBOUR
   ARBOUR
THREE
T  REE
T  REE
   ARBOUR
   TREE
   ARBOUR
 HARBOUR
THREE
   ARBOUR
   TREE
   ARBOUR
THREE
 HARBOUR
   TREE
   ARBOUR
T  REE
T  REE
THREE
   ARBOUR
 HARBOUR
 HARBOUR
   ARBOUR
THREE
T  REE
T  REE
```

```
leaf    love
 leaf   love
  leaf  love
   leaflove
    lealove
     ledove
      leafe
       lexf
       lduaf
       loreaf
       lovleaf
       loveleaf
       love leaf
       love  leaf
       love   leaf
```

```
FOREST FOREST FOREST FOREST FOREST FOREST FOREST FOREST
FOREST FOREST FOREST FOREST FOREST FOREST FOREST FOREST
FOREST FOREST FOREST FOREST FOREST FOREST FOREST FOREST
firEST FOREST FOREST FOREST FOREST FOREST FOREST FOREST
firfir FOREST FOREST FOREST FOREST FOREST FOREST FOREST
firfir firEST FOREST FOREST FOREST FOREST FOREST FOREST
firfir firfir FOREST FOREST FOREST FOREST FOREST FOREST
firfir firfir firEST FOREST FOREST FOREST FOREST FOREST
firfir firfir firfir FOREST FOREST FOREST FOREST FOREST
firfir firfir firfir firEST FOREST FOREST FOREST FOREST
firfir firfir firfir firfir FOREST FOREST FOREST FOREST
firfir firfir firfir firfir firEST FOREST FOREST FOREST
firfir firfir firfir firfir firfir FOREST FOREST FOREST
firfir firfir firfir firfir firfir firEST FOREST FOREST
firfir firfir firfir firfir firfir firfir FOREST FOREST
firfir firfir firfir firfir firfir firfir firEST FOREST
firfir firfir firfir firfir firfir firfir firfir FOREST
```

```
        m    o

       .n    o


        n.   m


        o    o


        o    n.


        o    m


        o    o


        m    n.
```

if

if

l if t

if

if

if

if

if

if

if

if

if

if

if

if

if

if

if

```
            M
            O
            N
            D
            R       H
    F I N L A Y
            A   M
    I A N   I A N
            L
            T
        M O N D R I A N
            N       A
                    N       M
                H A M I L T O N
                    A       N
                    I A N   D
                            R
                            I
                            A
                            N
```

mondr ian hamilton finlay

```
marilyn m ro  mari n m ro
   l  on e    ly  on e
marilyn m ro  mari n m ro
   l  on e    ly  on e
marilyn m ro  mari n m ro
   l  on e    ly  on e
marilyn m ro  mari n m ro
   l  on e    ly  on e
marilyn m ro  mari n m ro
   l  on e    ly  on e
```

```
          s
          p i t
    c a t a p u l t
          i n   g   i
s t i n k         t t y
        k         e
        l i c k   l         s
            n     i n g a m
      g a g       e       a
        n         e u n u c h
        a         t       k
        l         e
                  r
                  e
                  d
```

erotic context ii

```
lov  e    st   ill
lov  lier st   ill
lov  lie  st   ill
lo        st
```

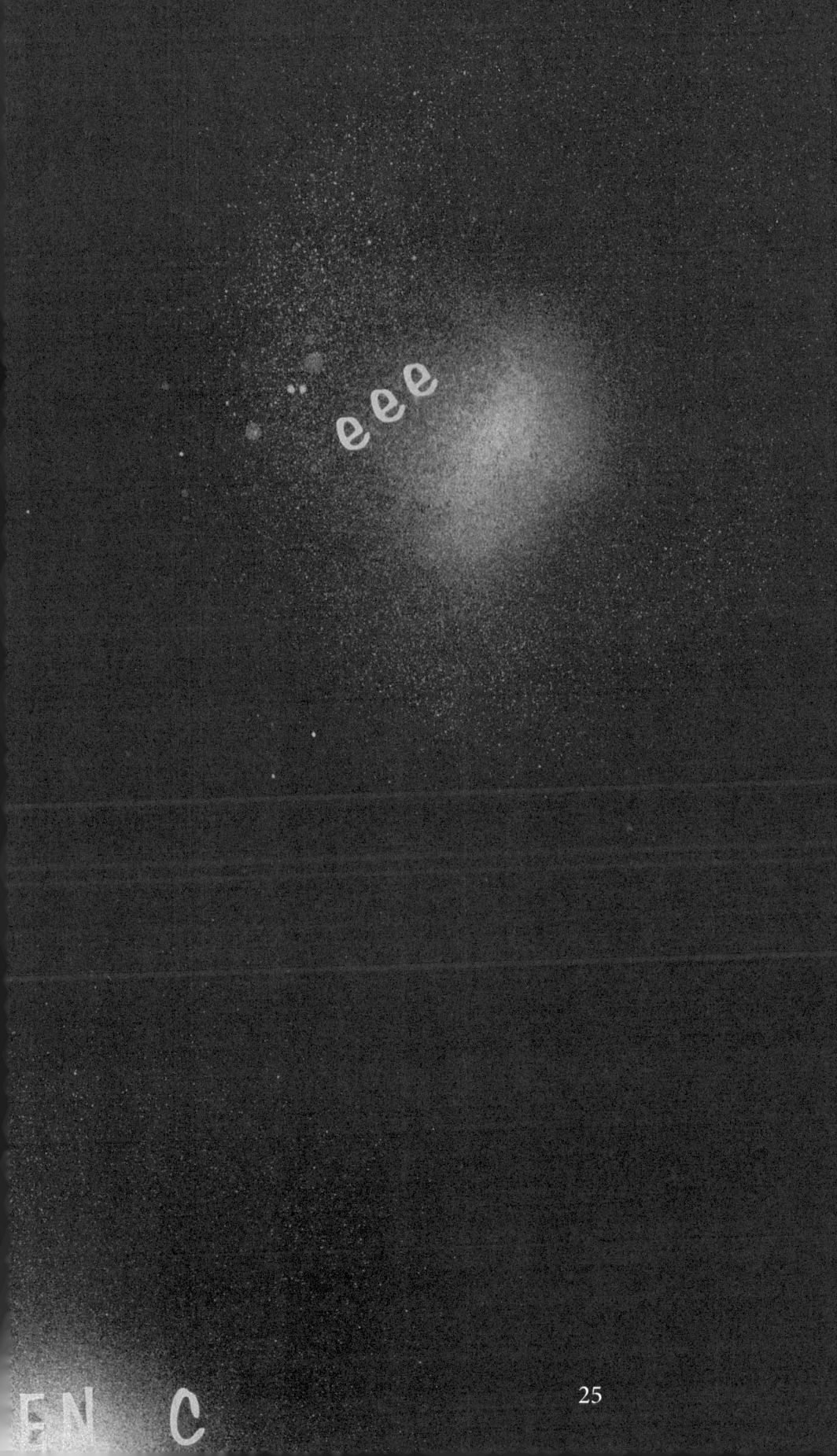

```
                                i
                                i
                                i
                                i
                                i
                                i
                                i
                                i
                                i
                                i
                                i
                                i
                                i
                                i
                                i
                                i
                                i
                p               i
                p               i
                p               i                                               s
                p               i                                               s
                p               i                                               s
                p               i                           e                   s
                p               i                           e                   s
                p               i                           e                   s
                p               i                           e                   s
   s            p               i                           e                   s
   s            p               i                           e                   s
   s            p               i                           e                   s
   s            p               i                           e                   s
   s            p               i           r               e                   s
```

TYPESTRACTS (1969-74)

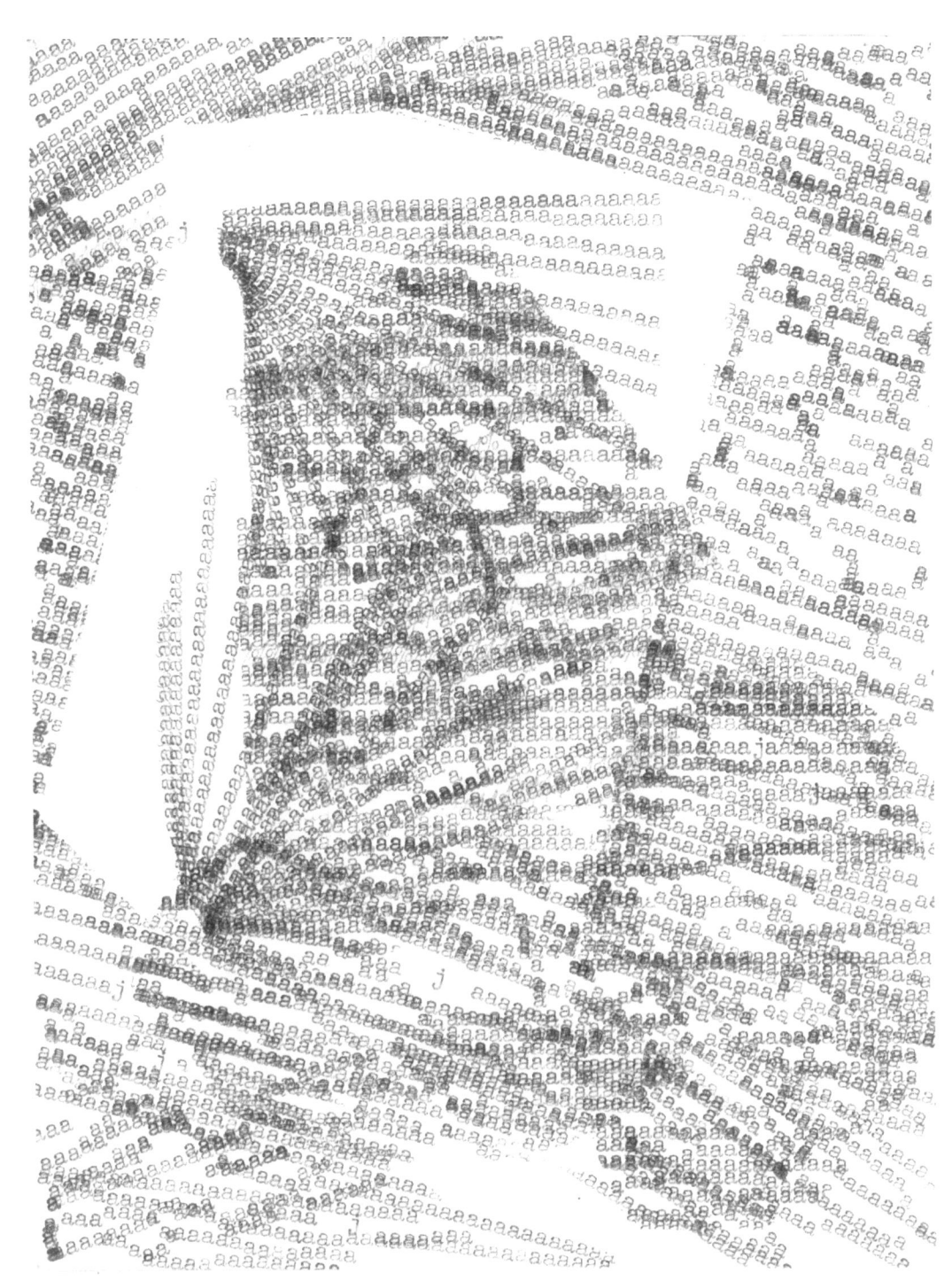

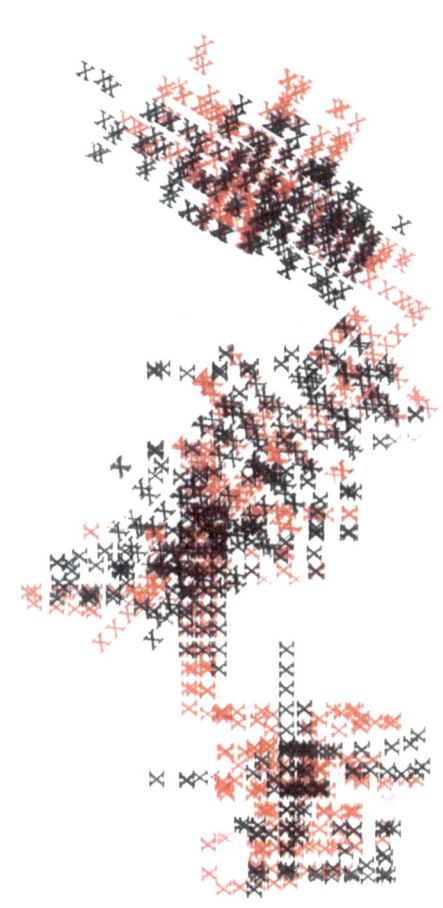

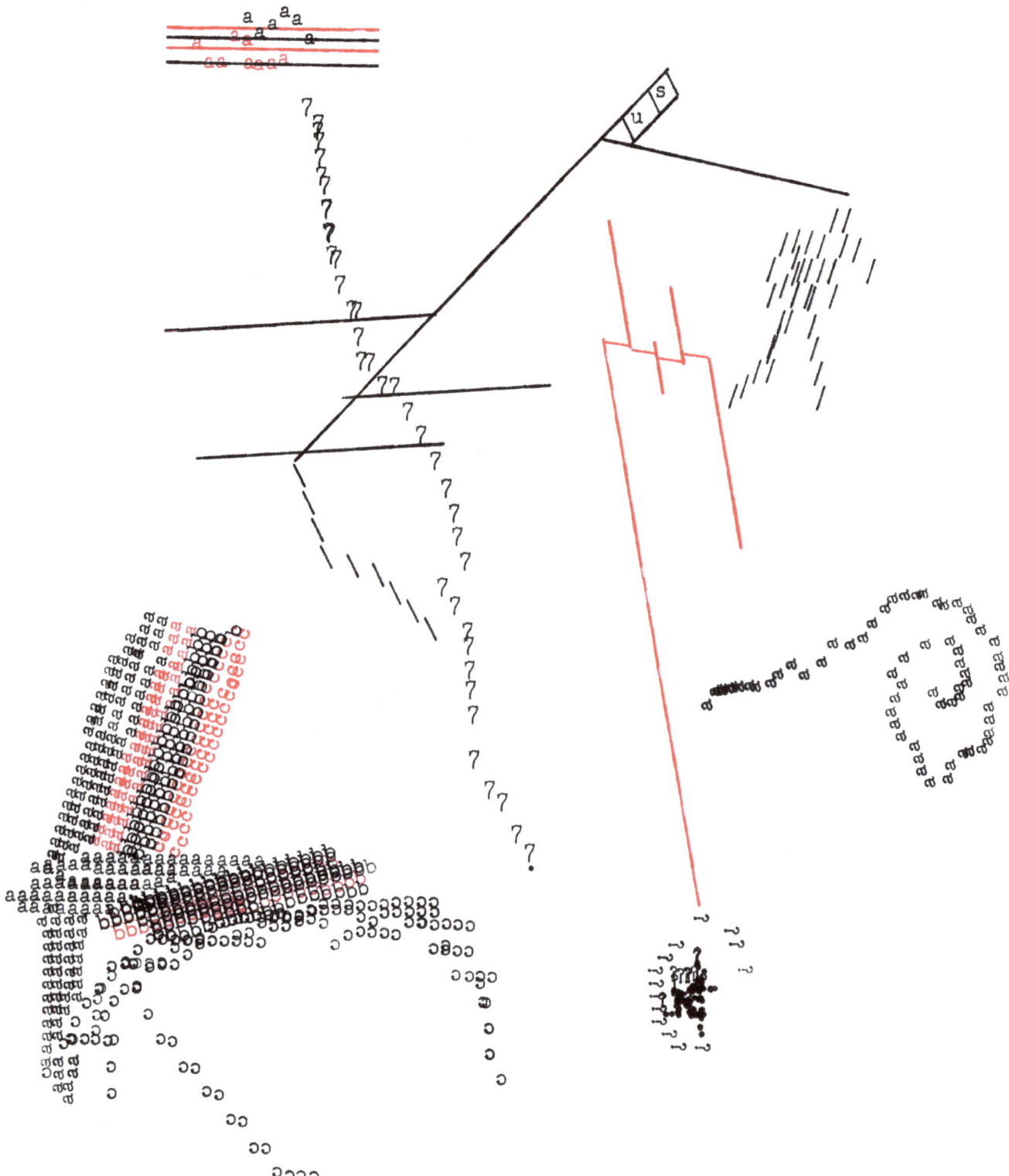

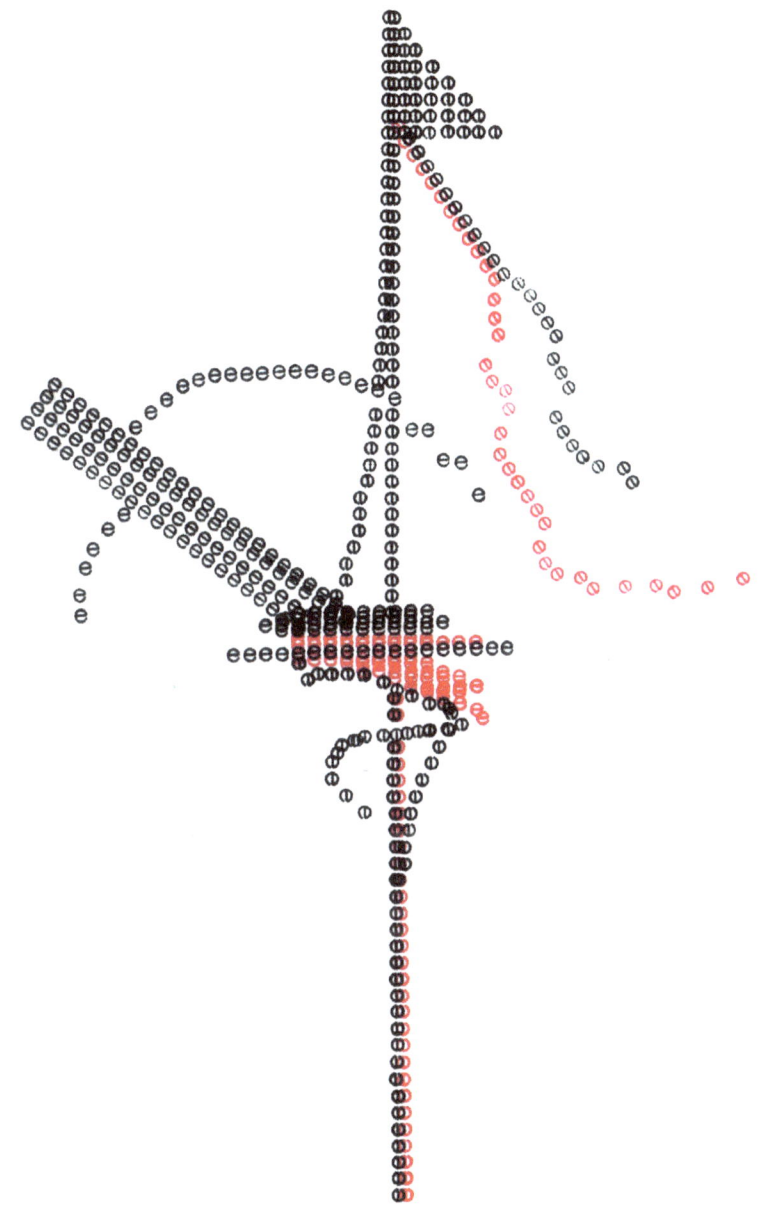

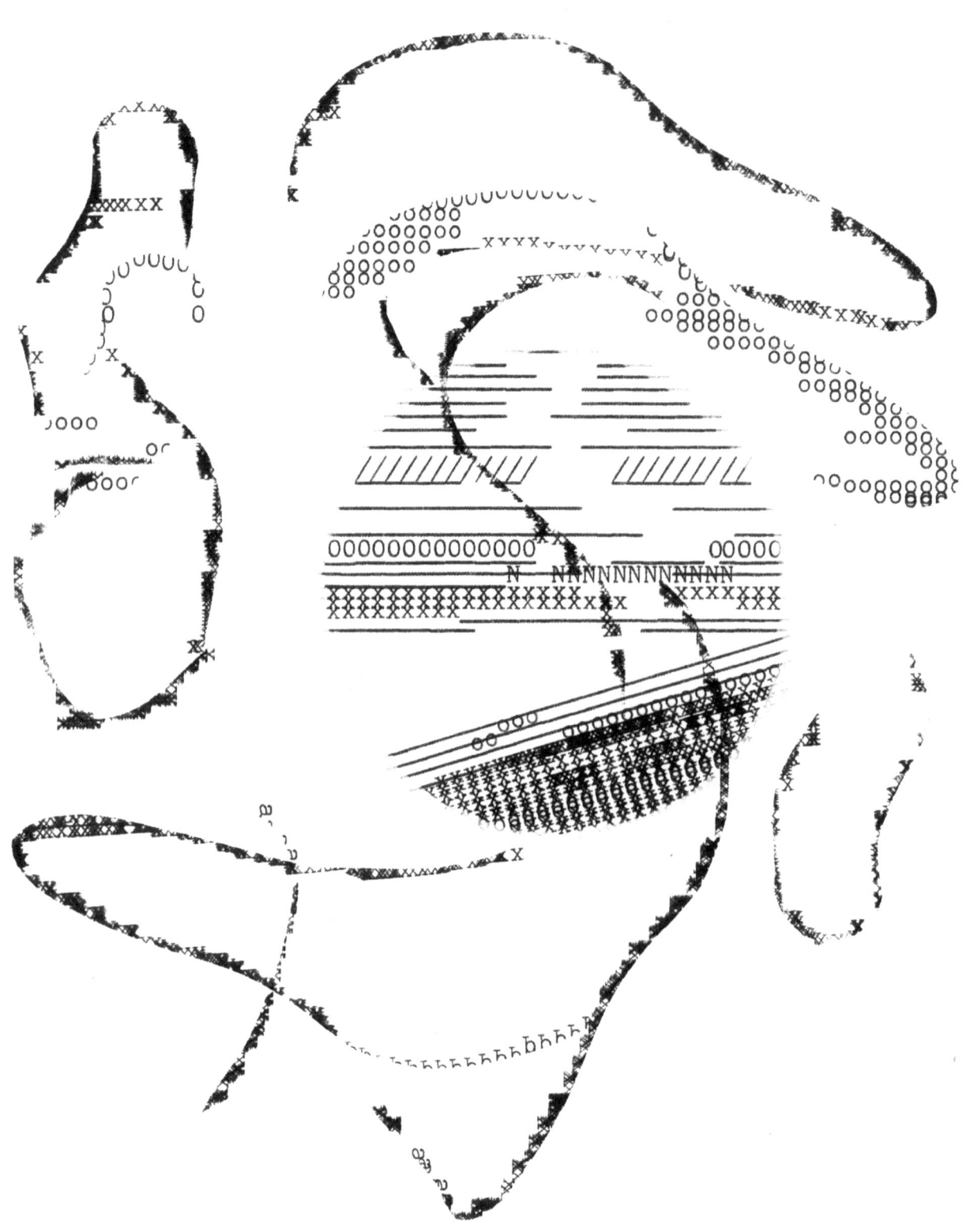

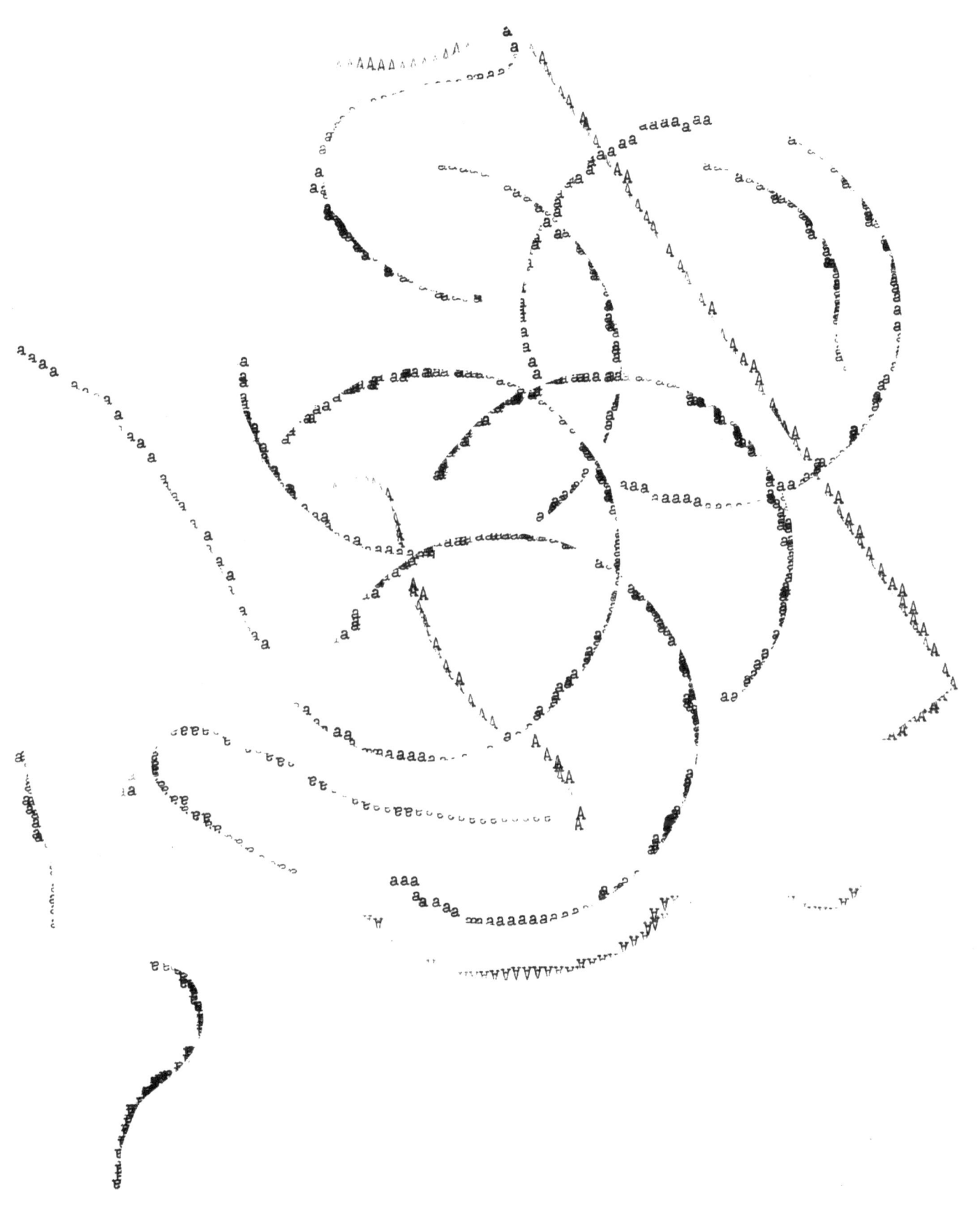

3 LETRASET POEMS (ca. 1975)

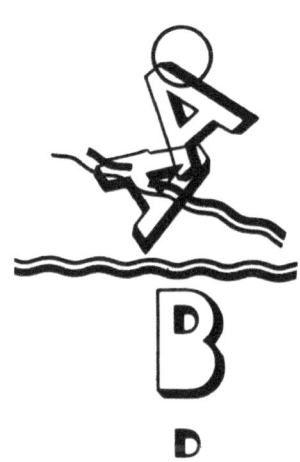

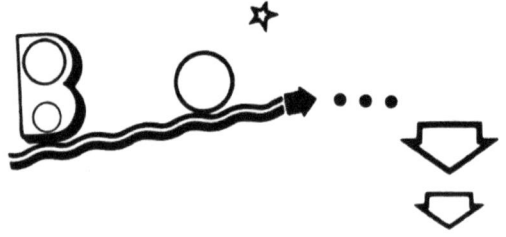

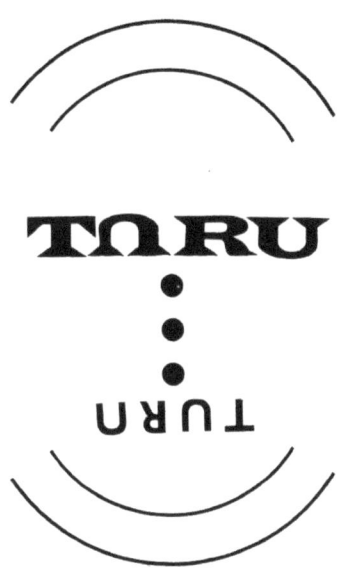

ORIGINS OF PROSE (1970)

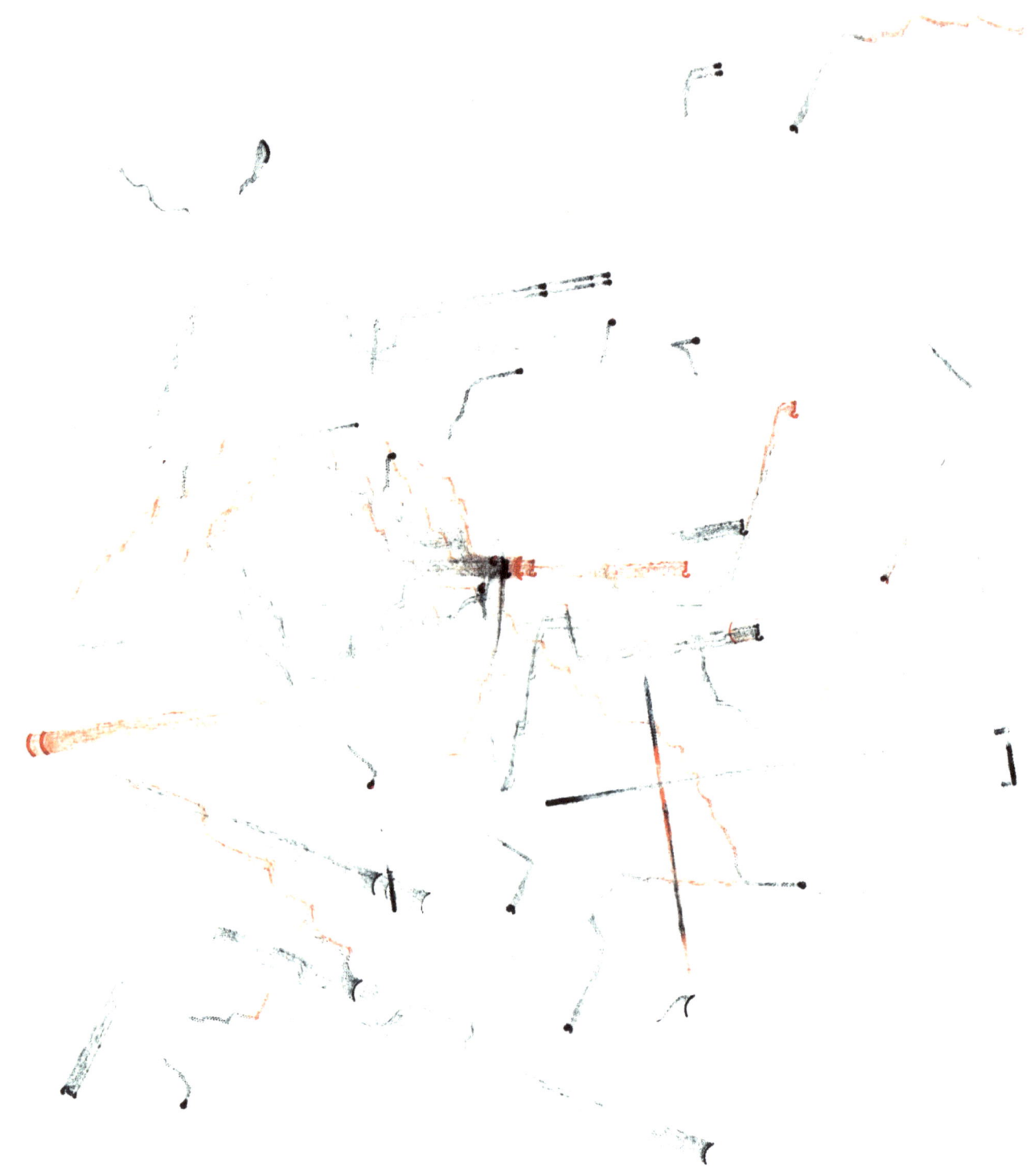

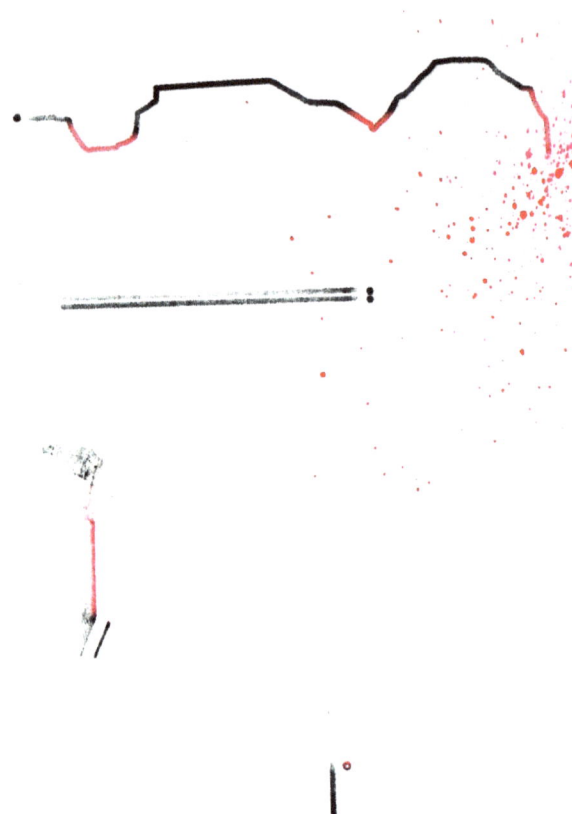

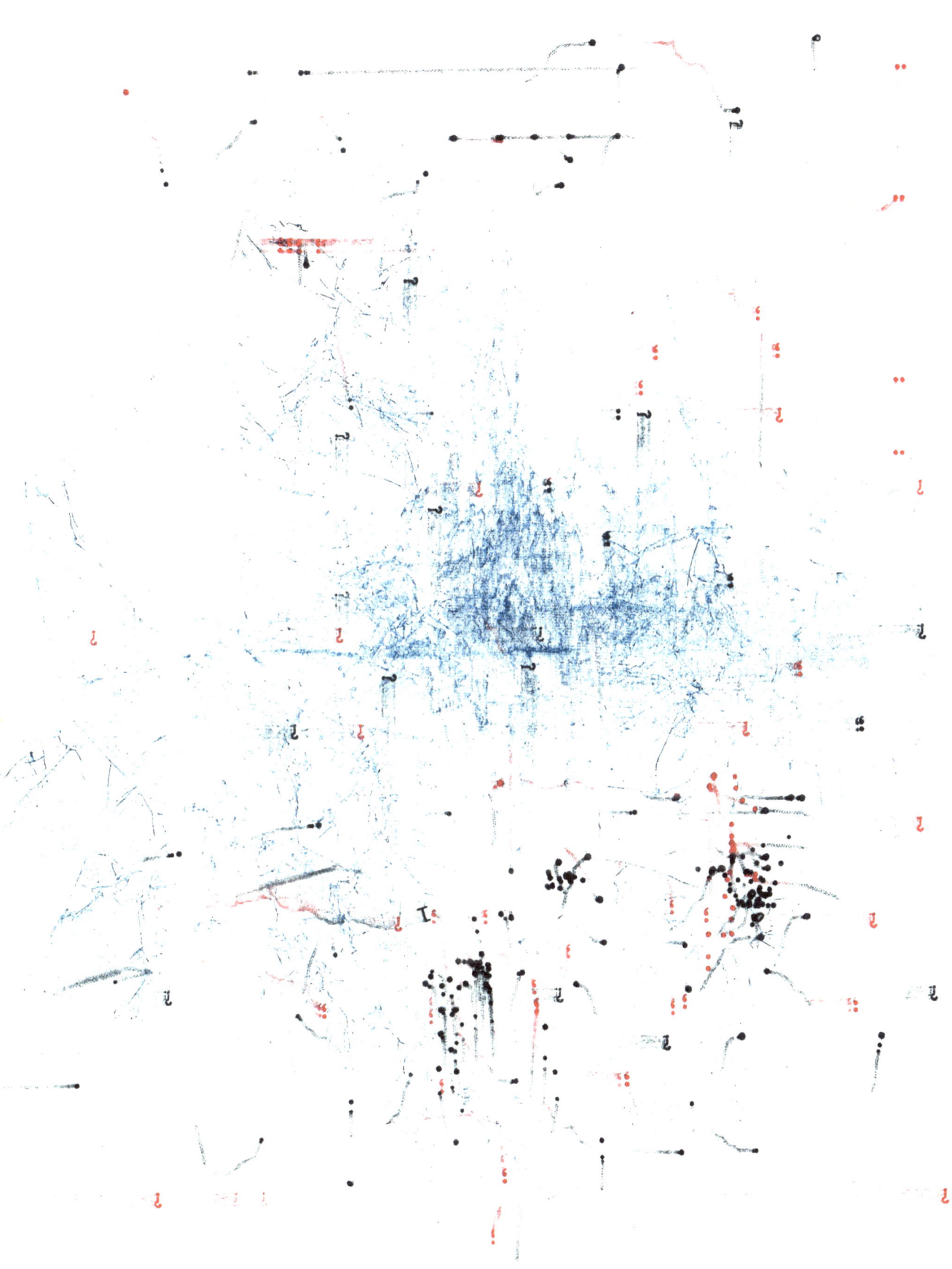

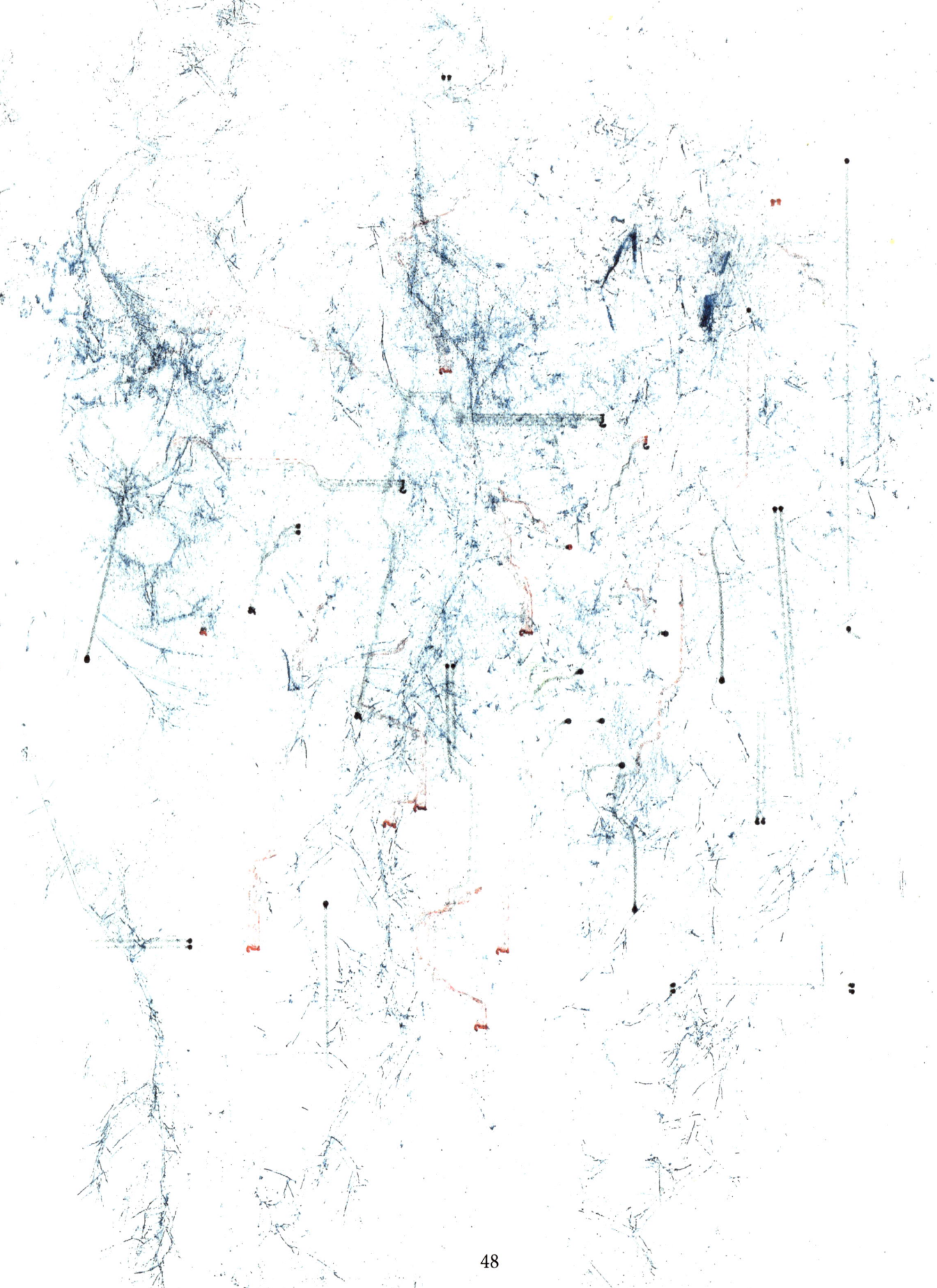

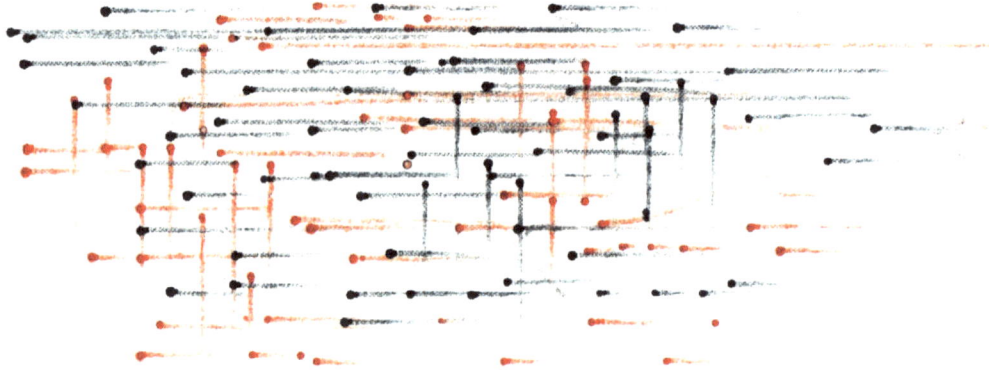

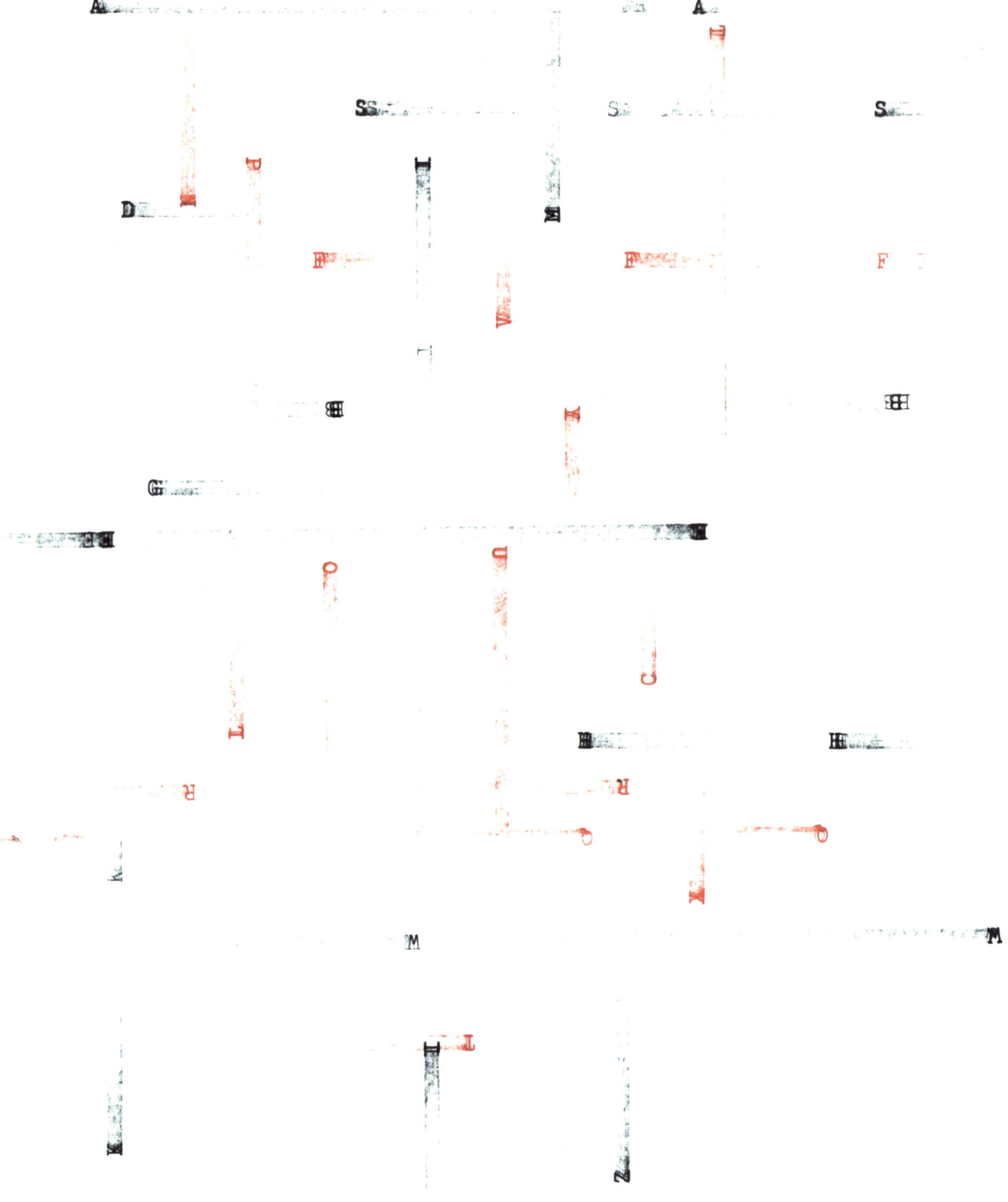

l   ght

2 SOUND POEMS (1970-73)

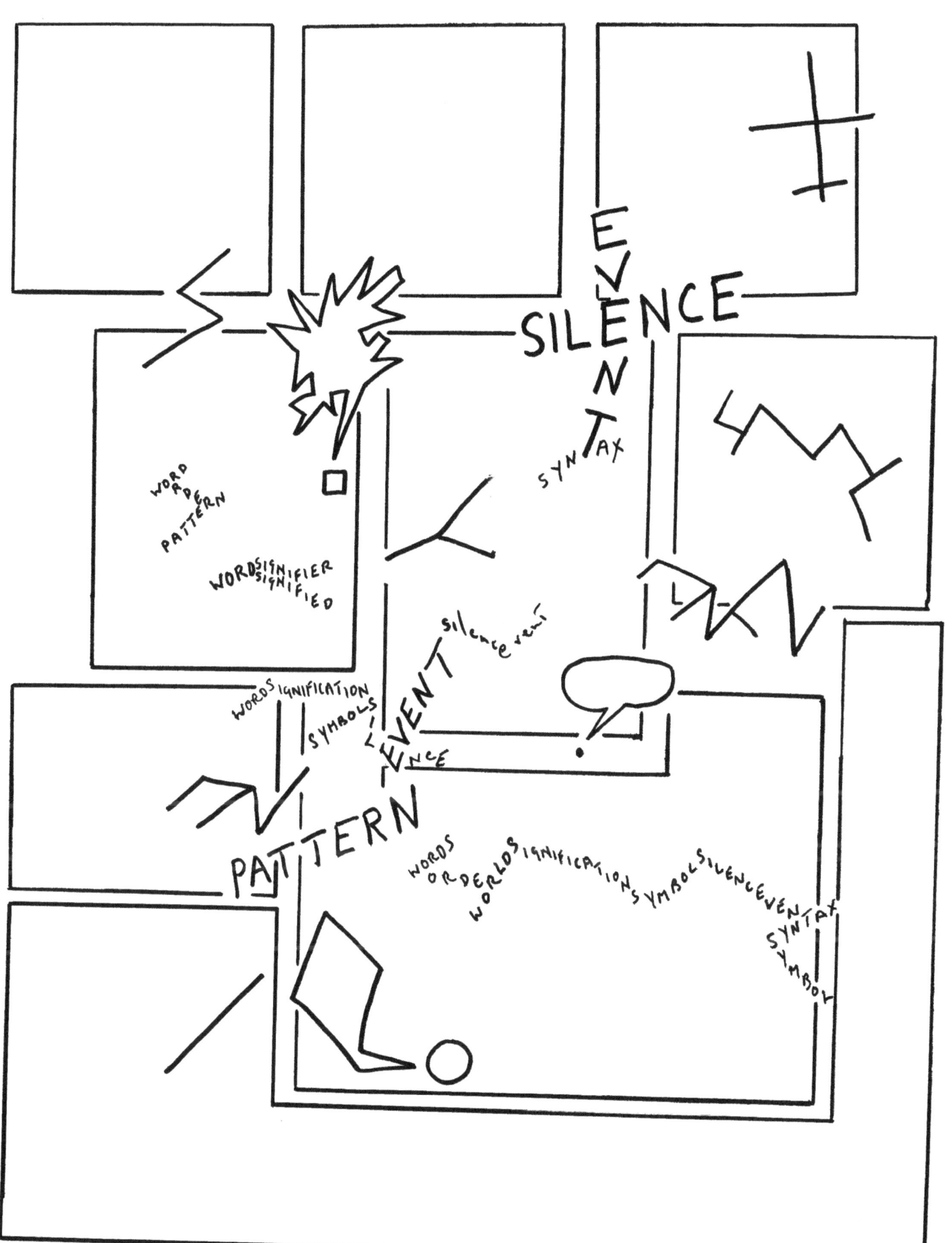

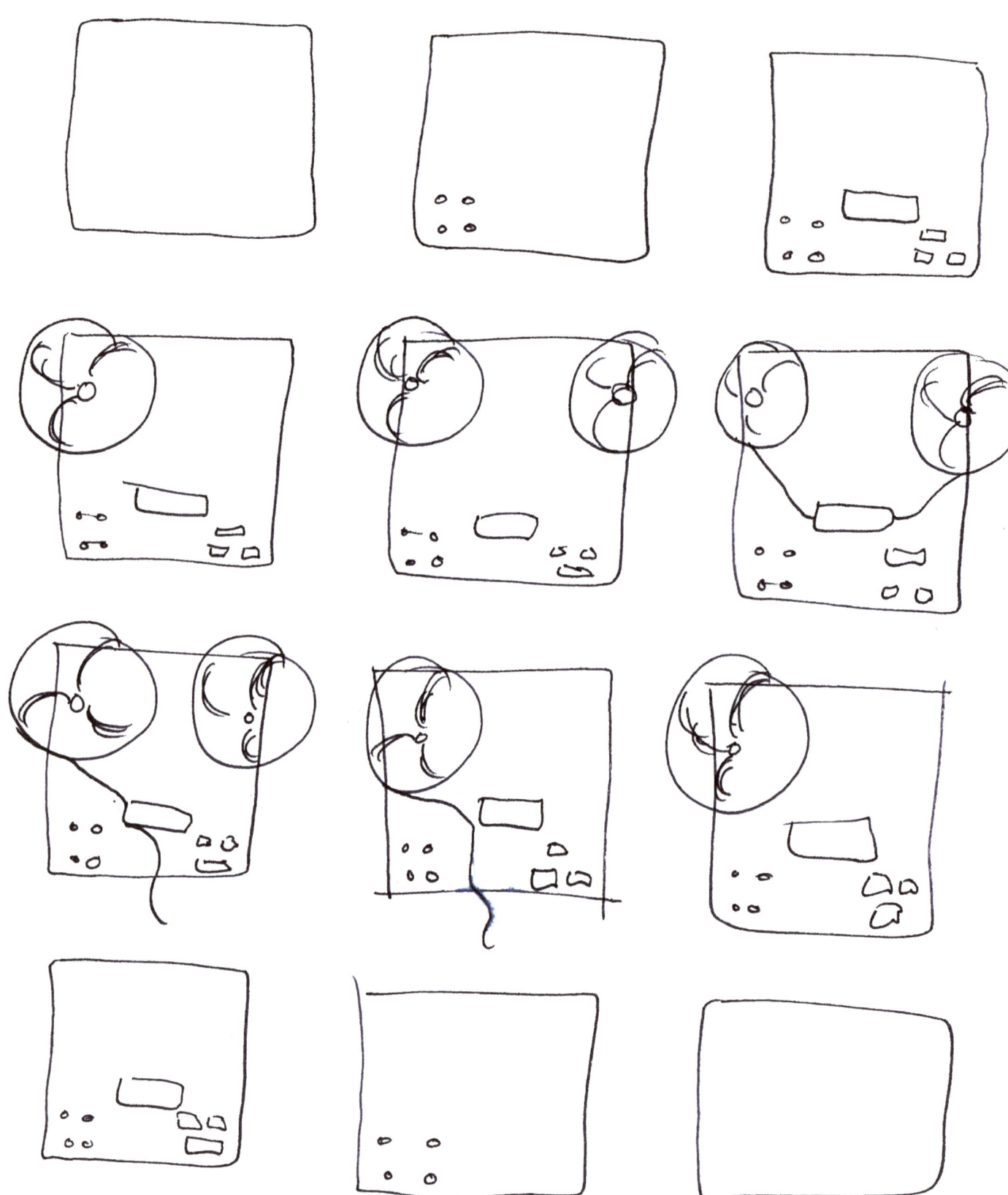

3 SEMIOTIC POEMS (1975, 1996)

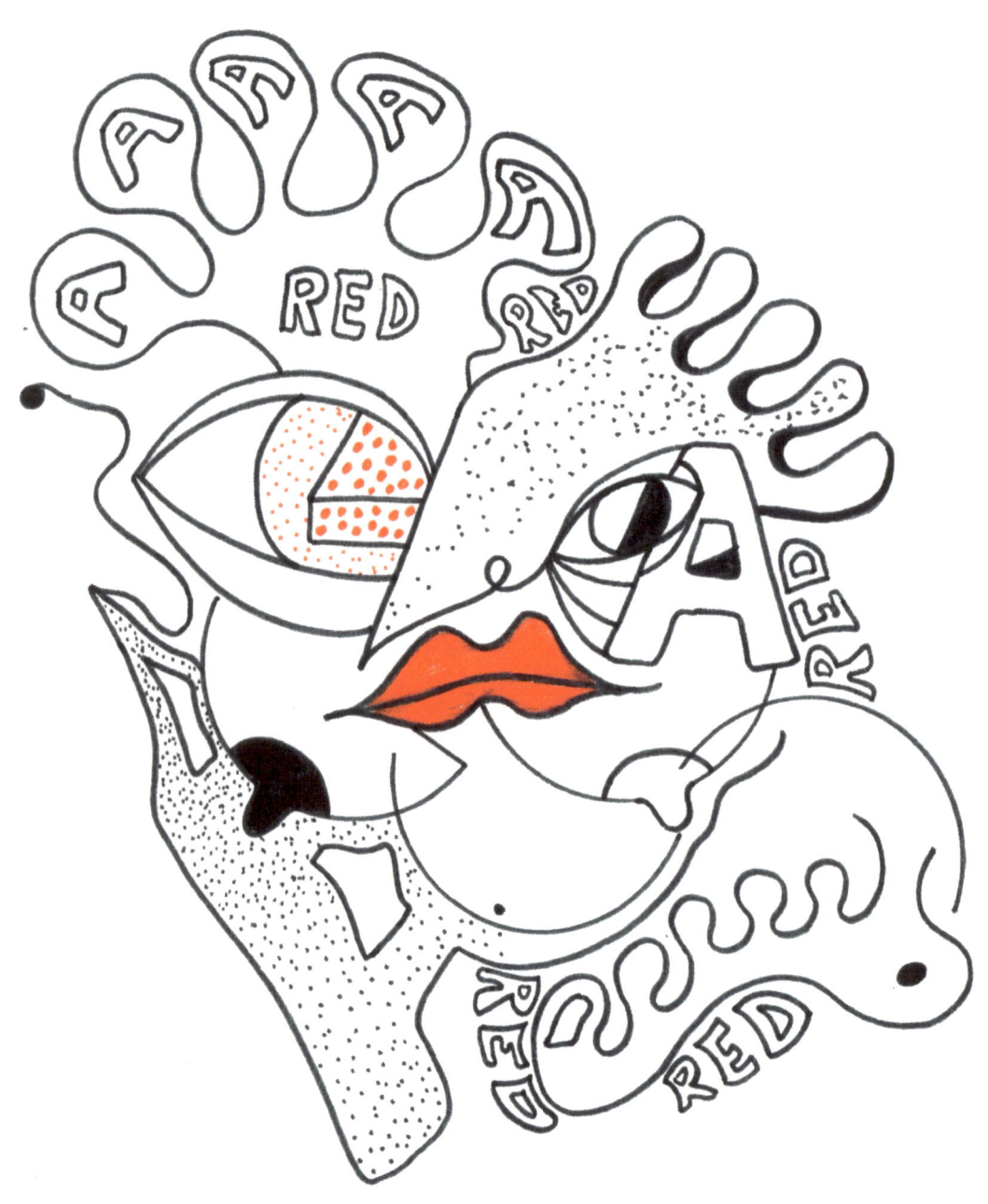

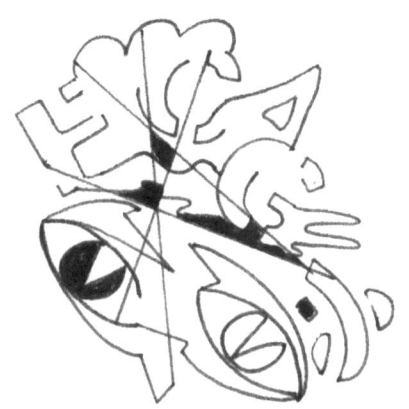

■ = speech
▽ = thought

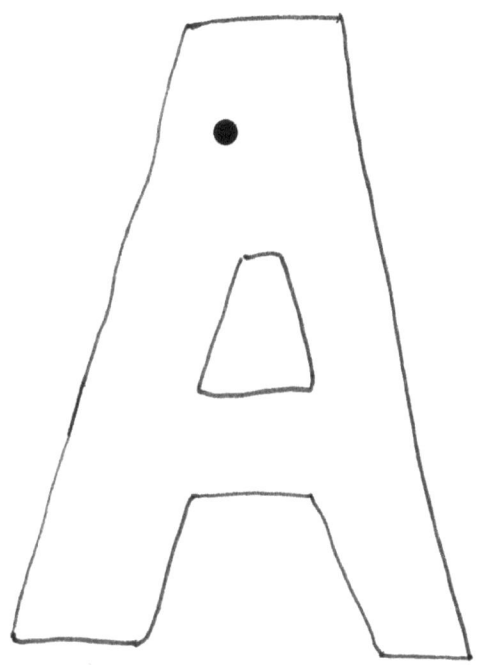

● = ink (gothic)
● = dot (baroque)
● = hole (postmodern)

MOON: A POST-SEMIOTIC SEQUENCE (1970)

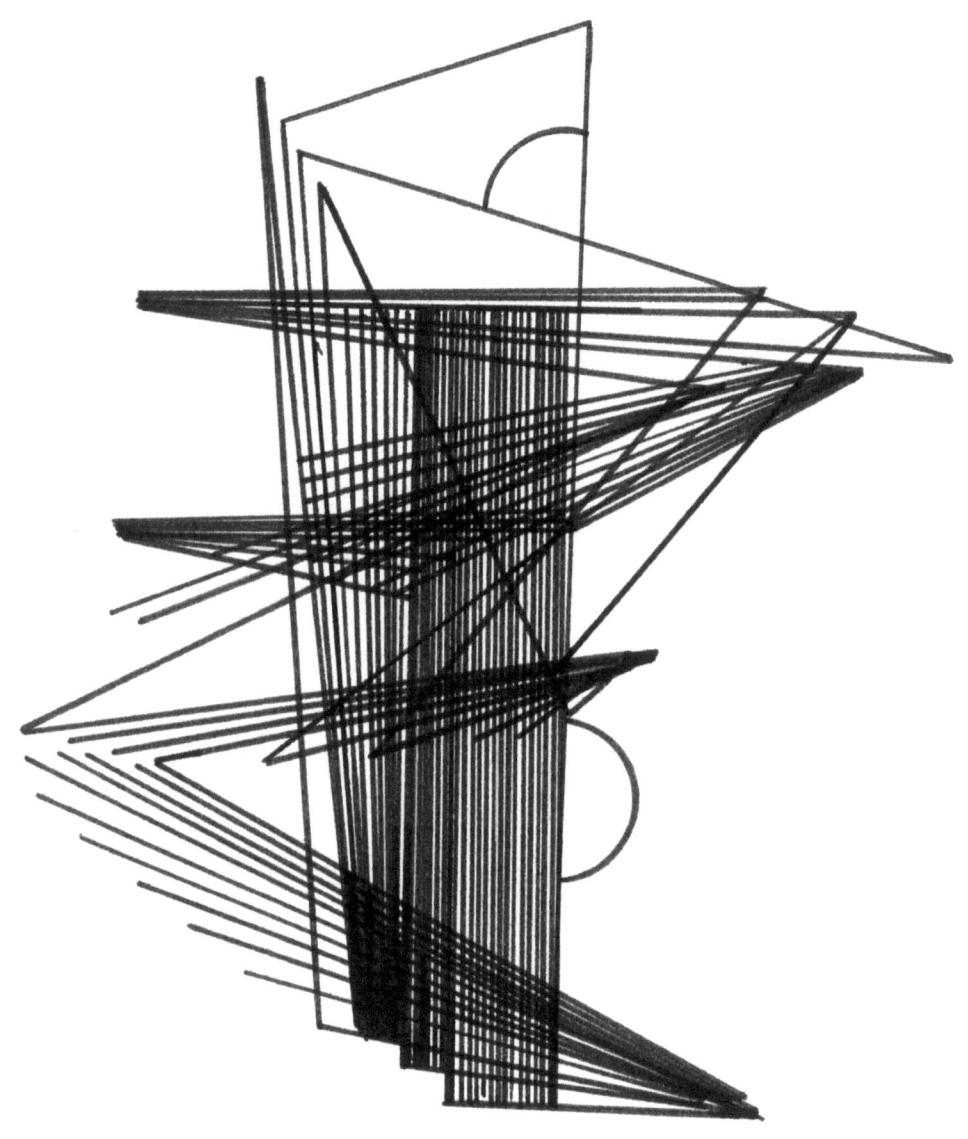

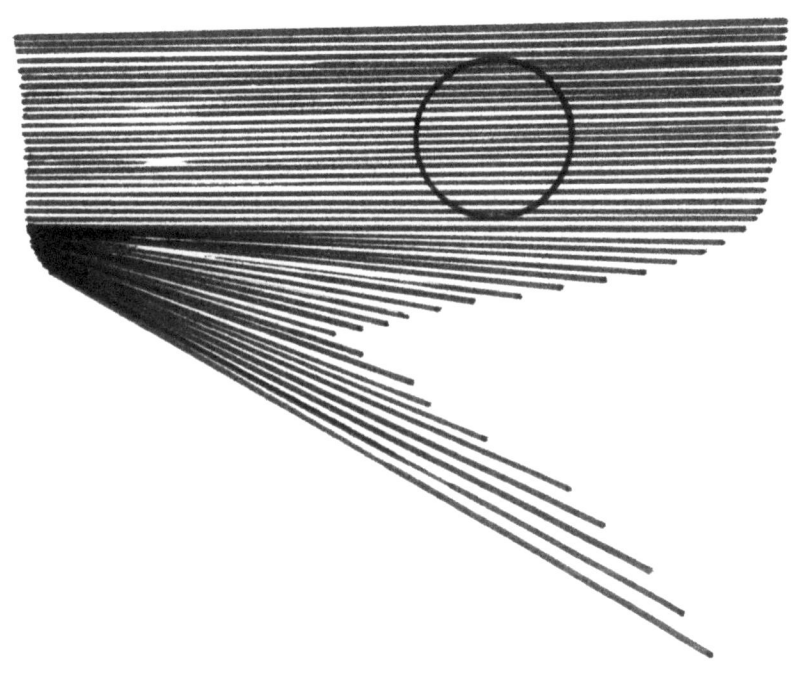

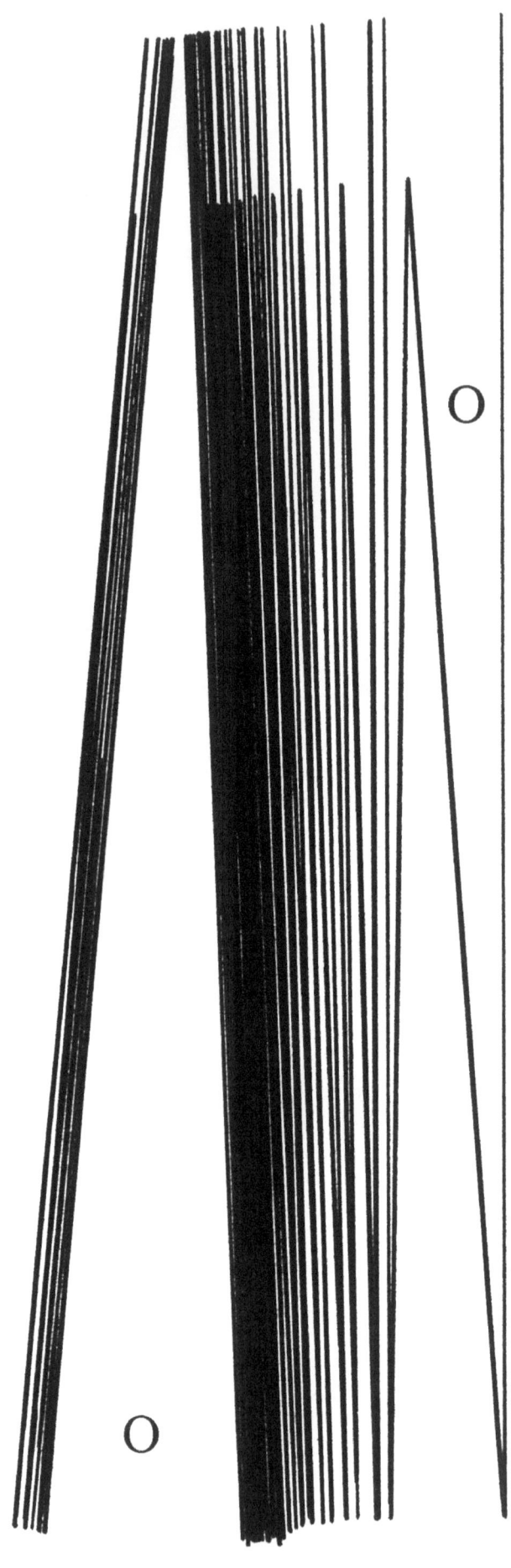

RUBBER STAMP POEMS (1969-70)

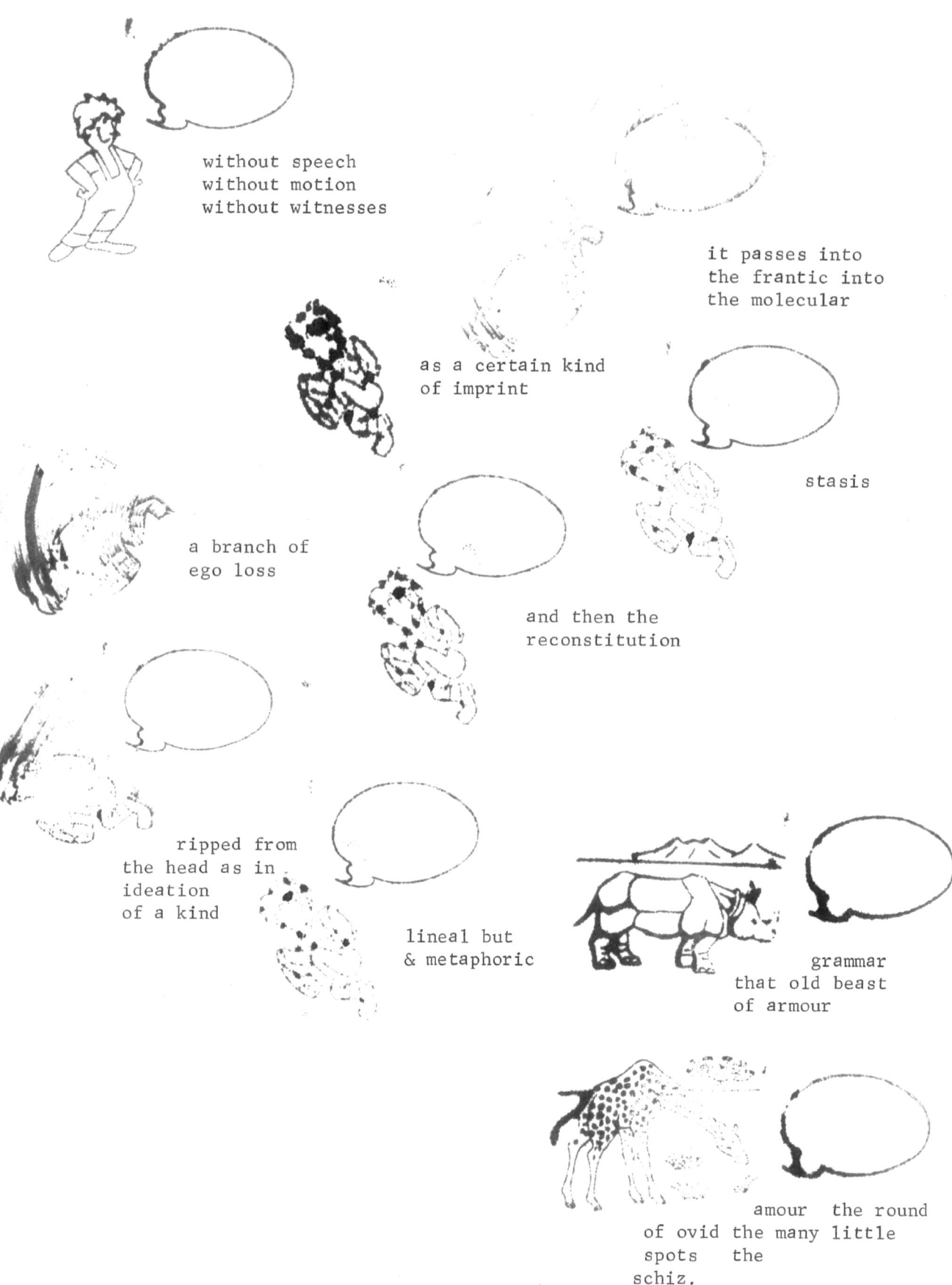

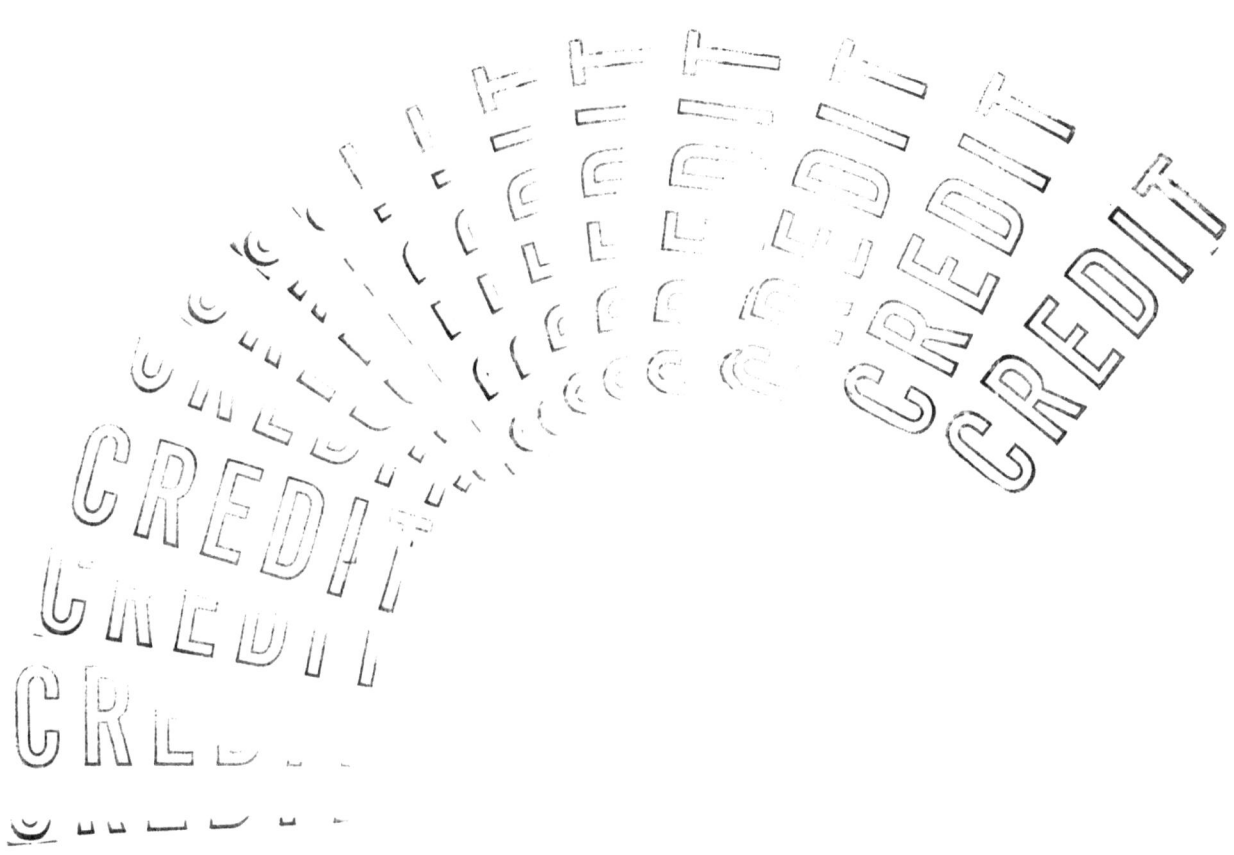

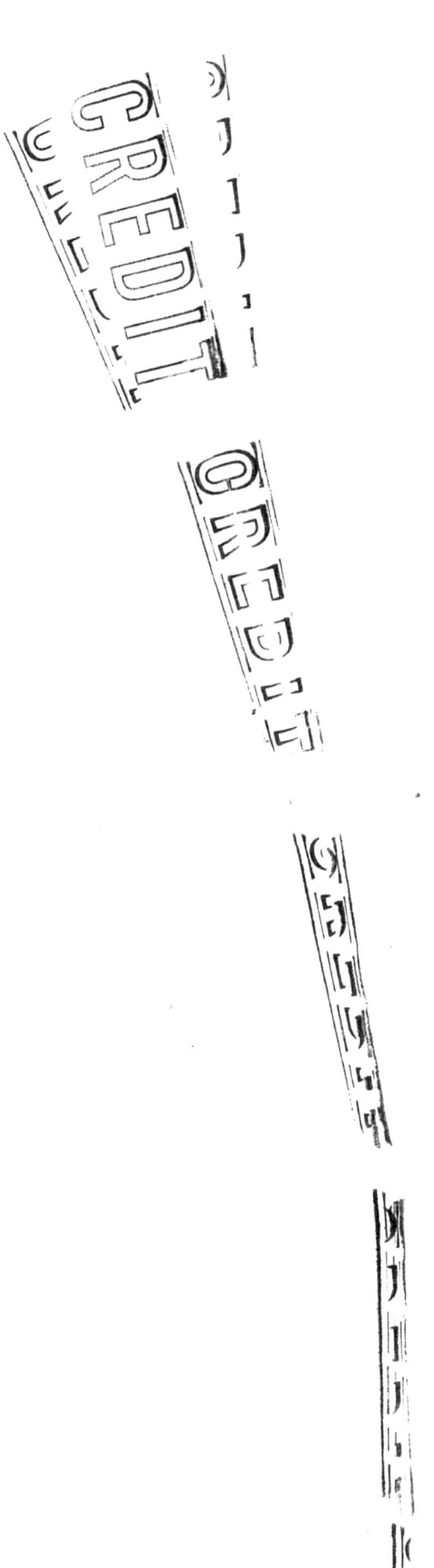

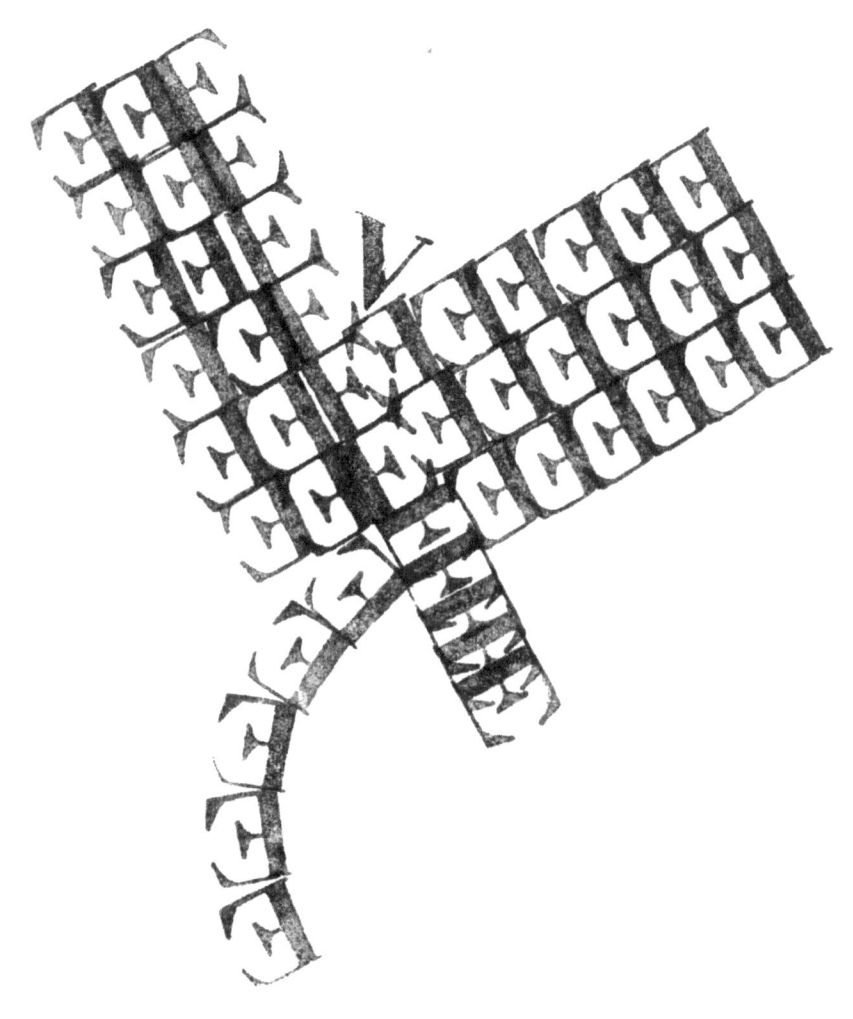

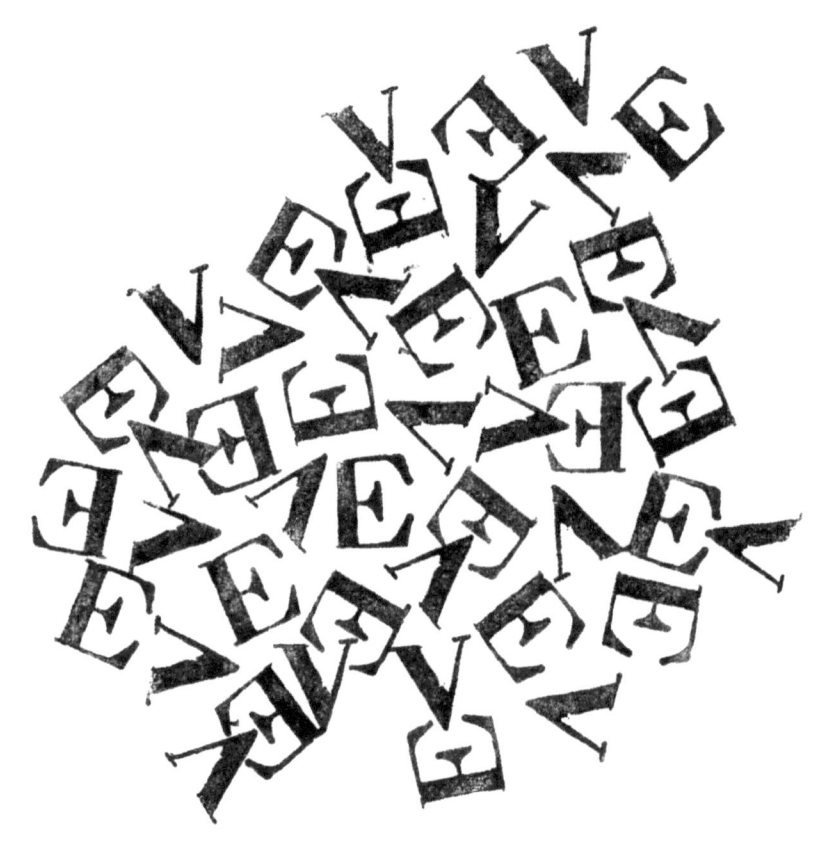

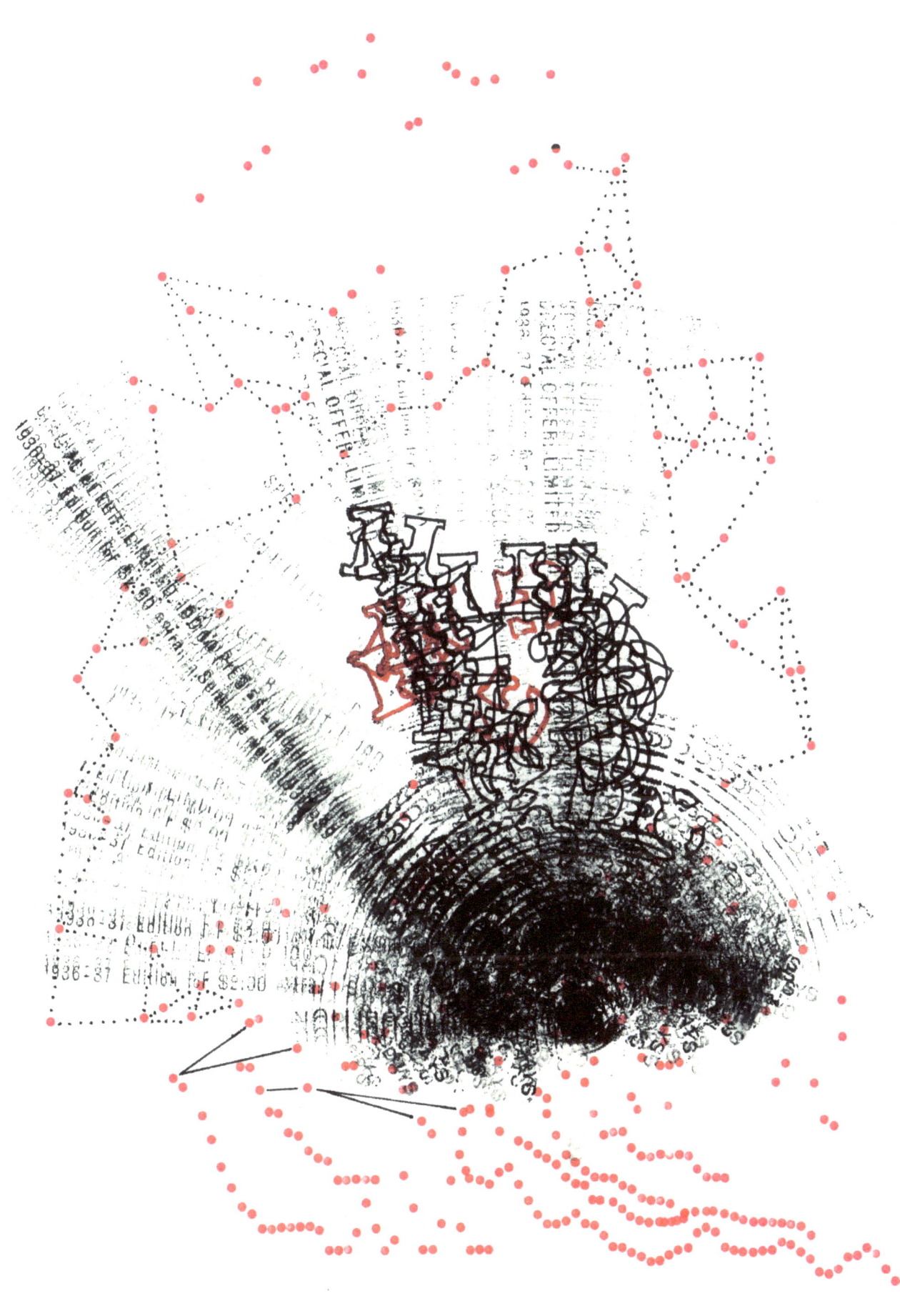

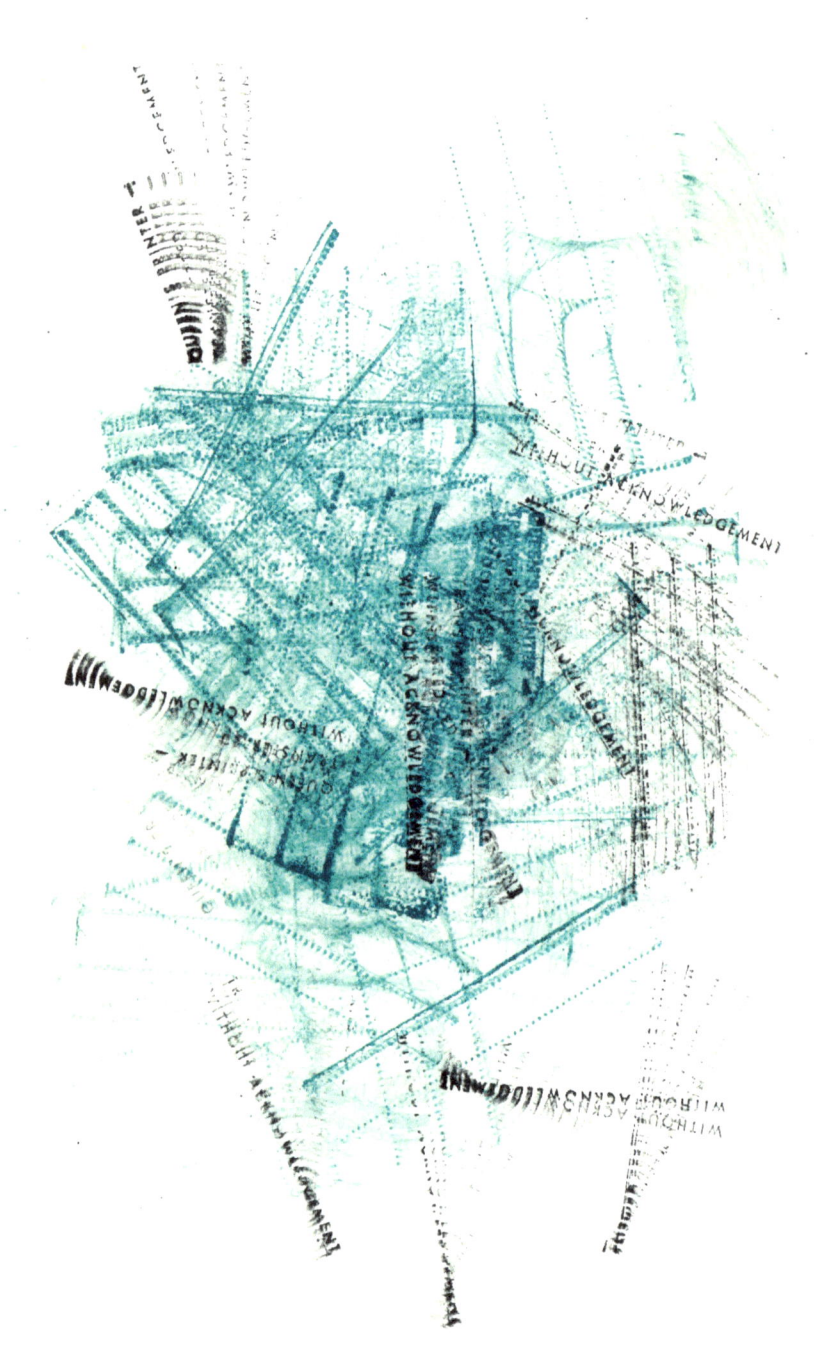

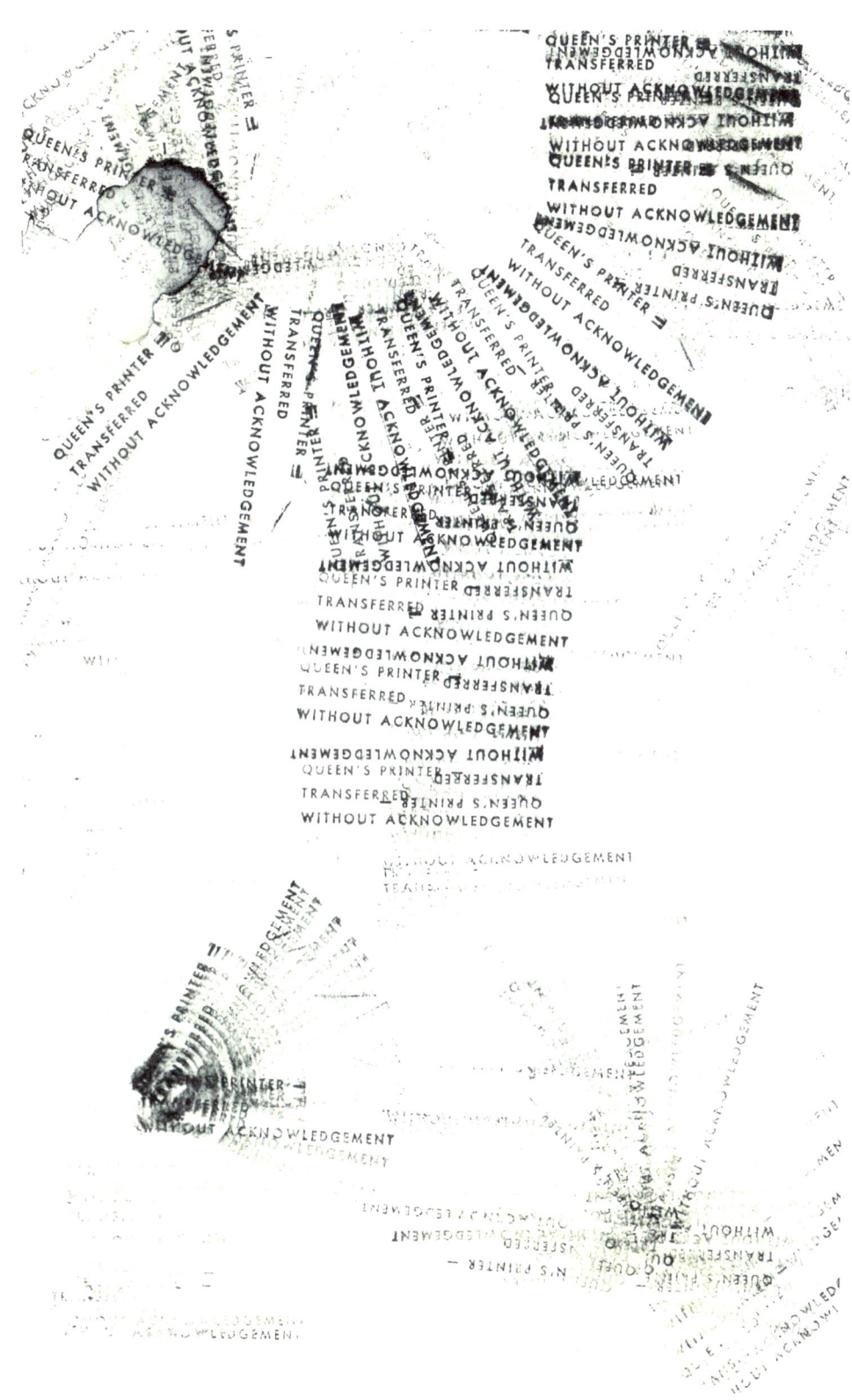

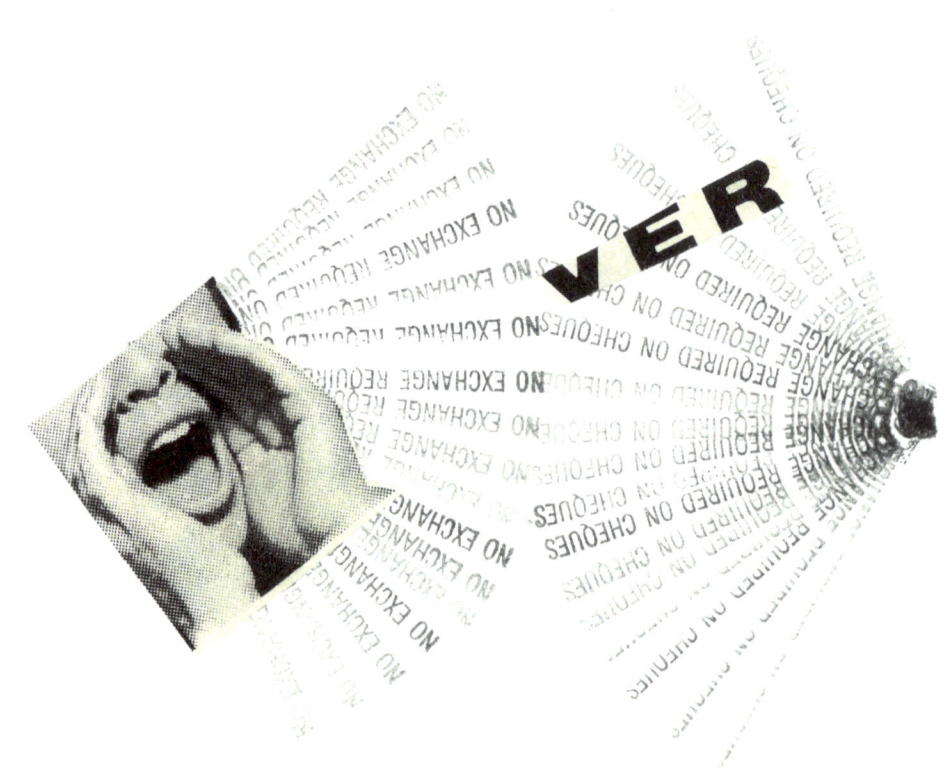

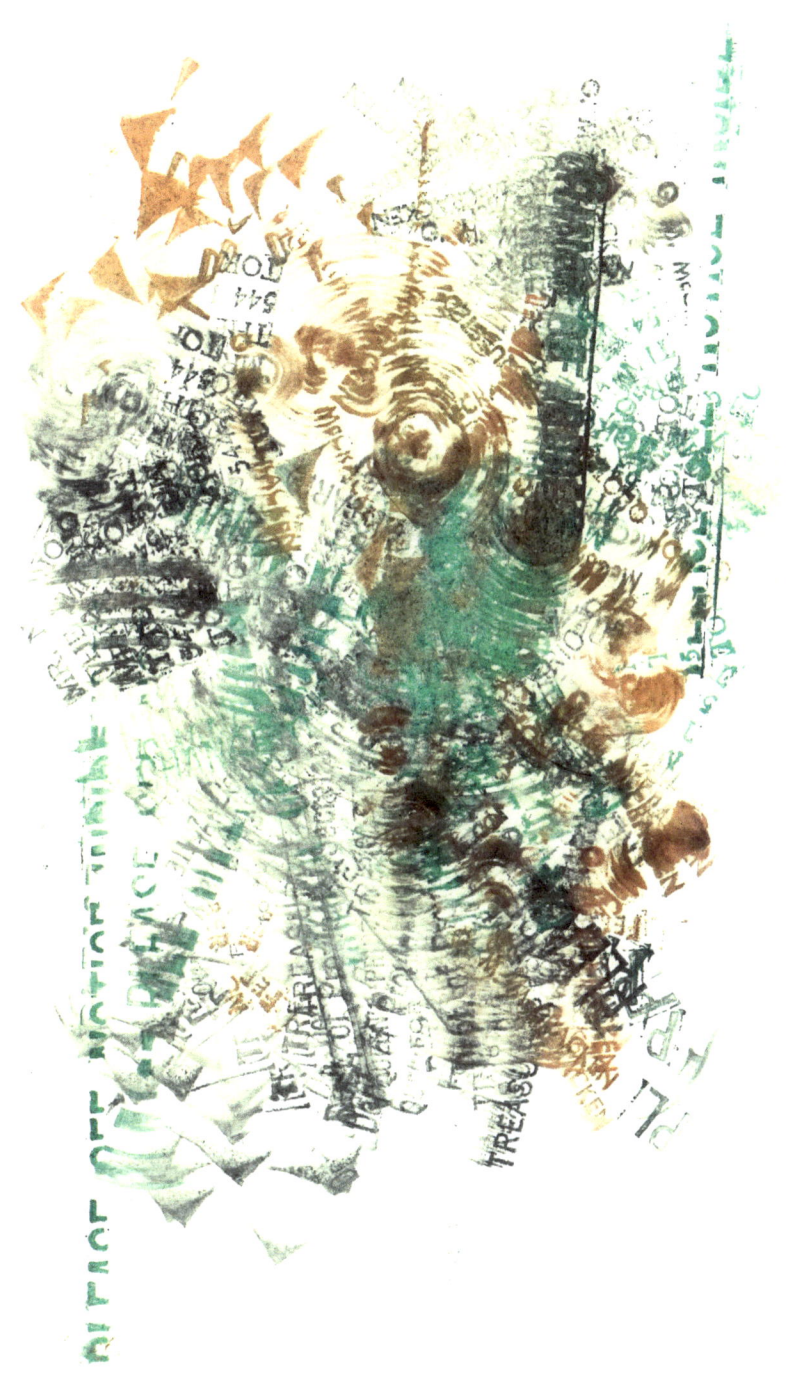

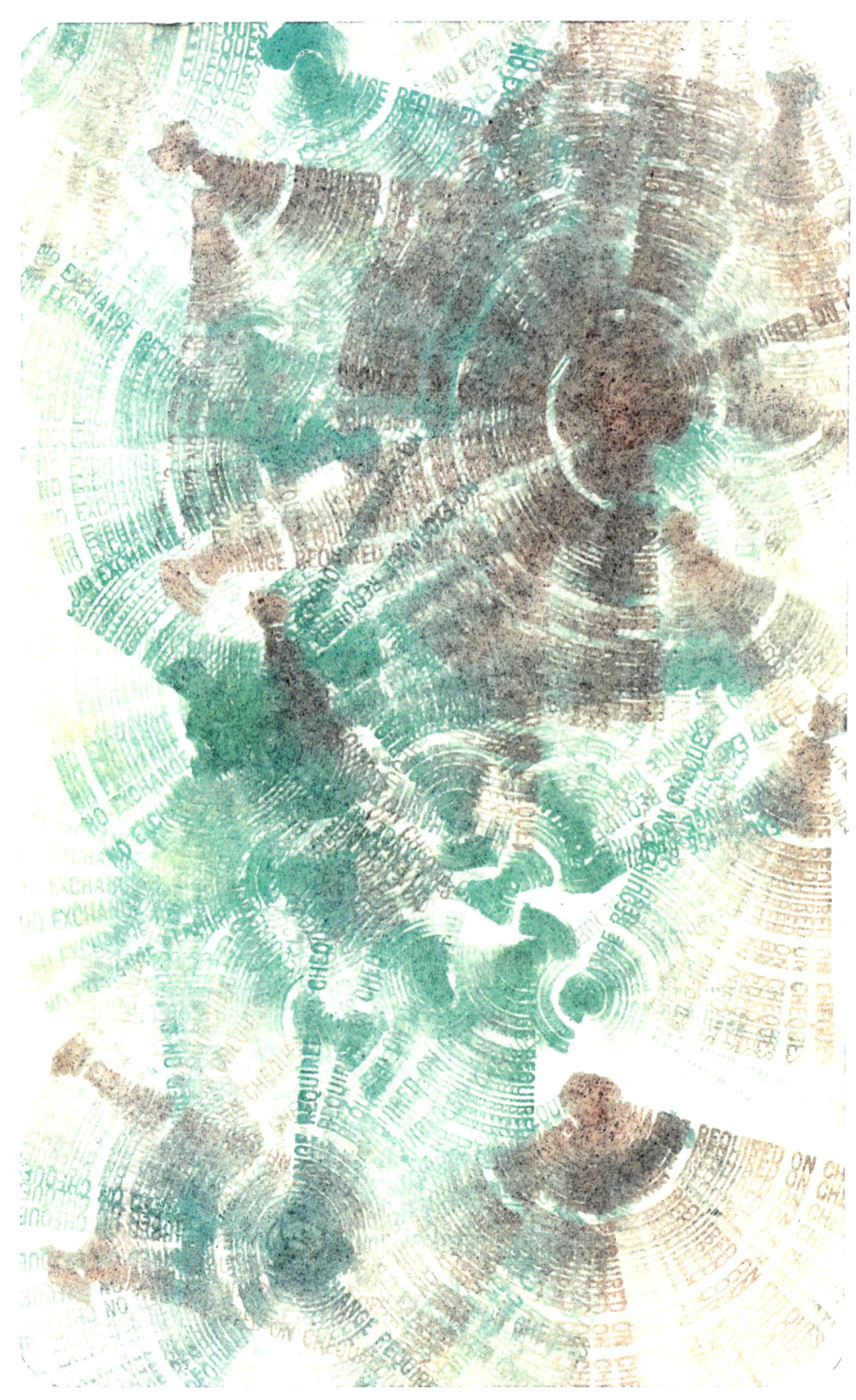

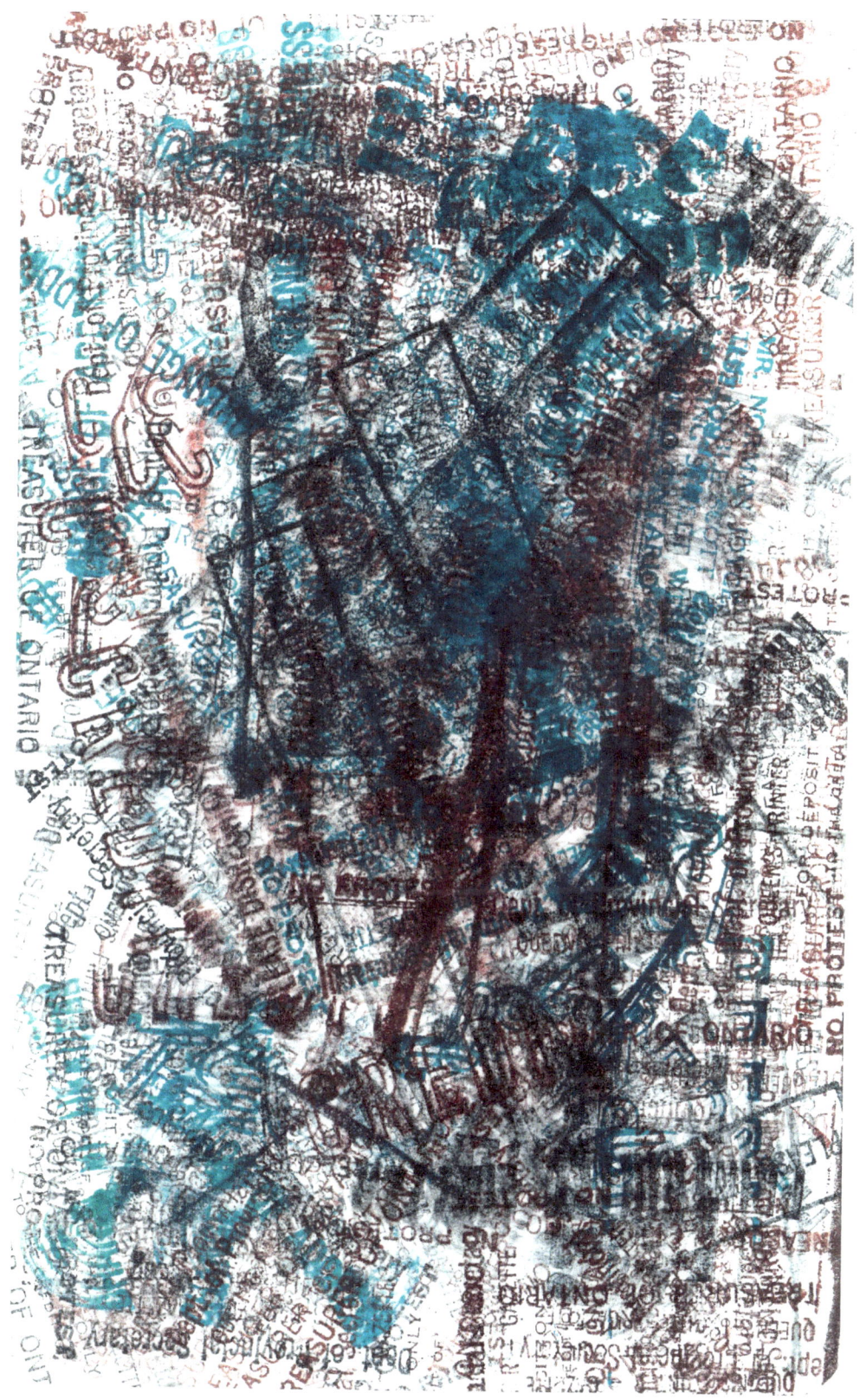

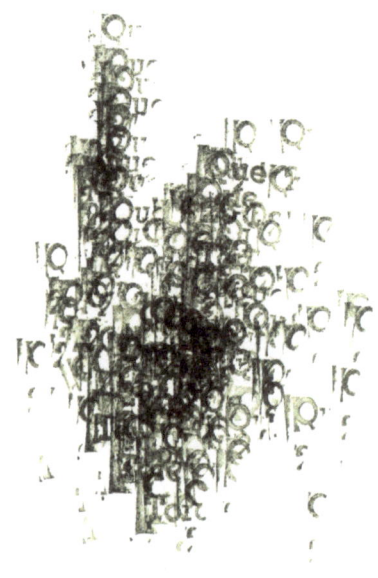

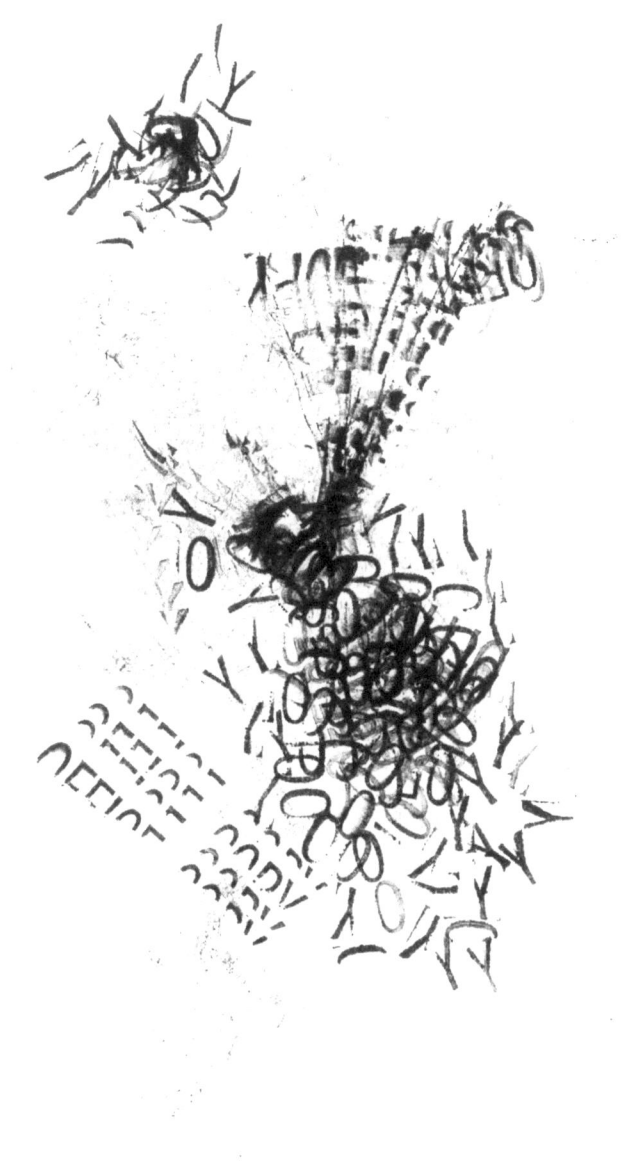

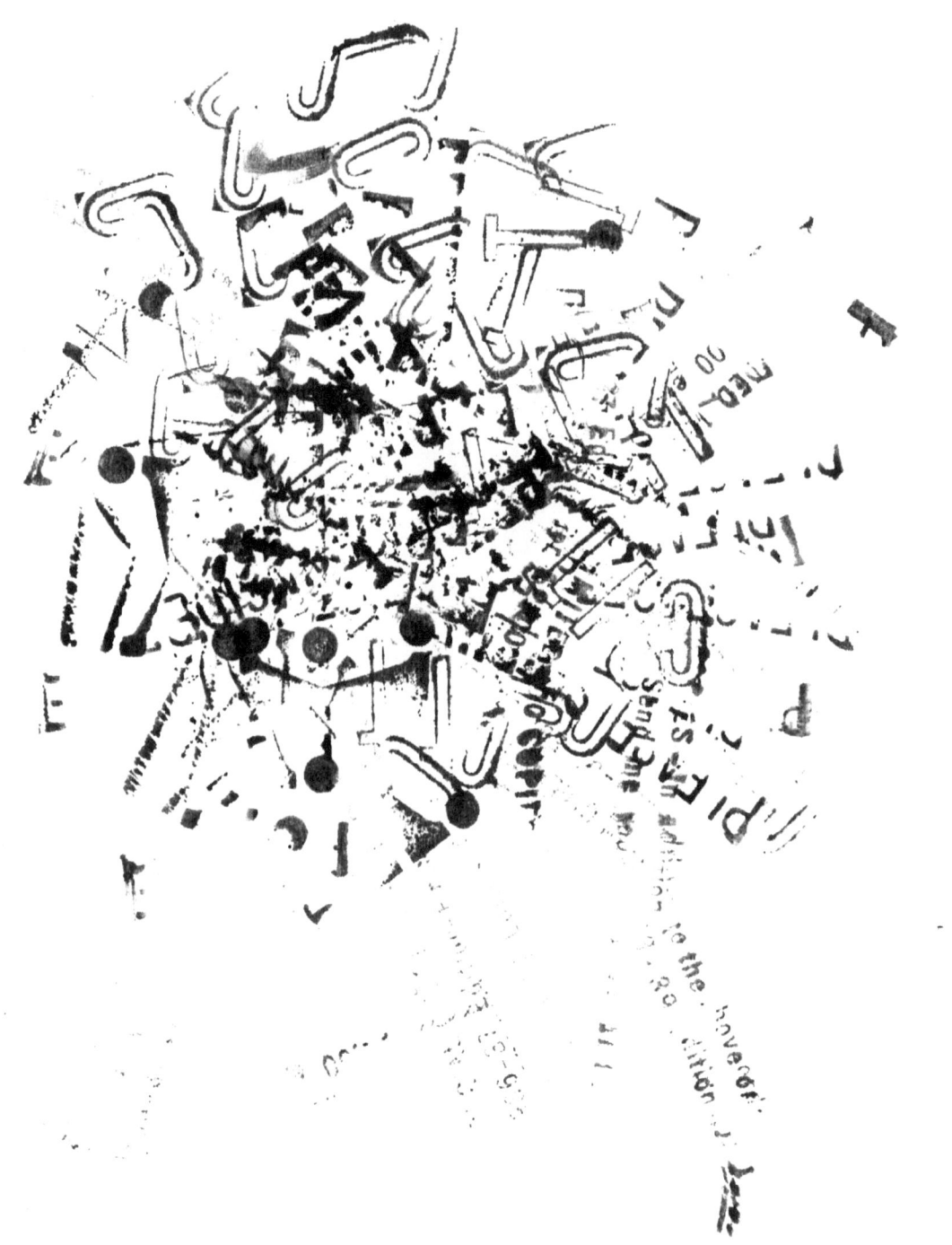

ON A THEORY OF MAYAN (1978)

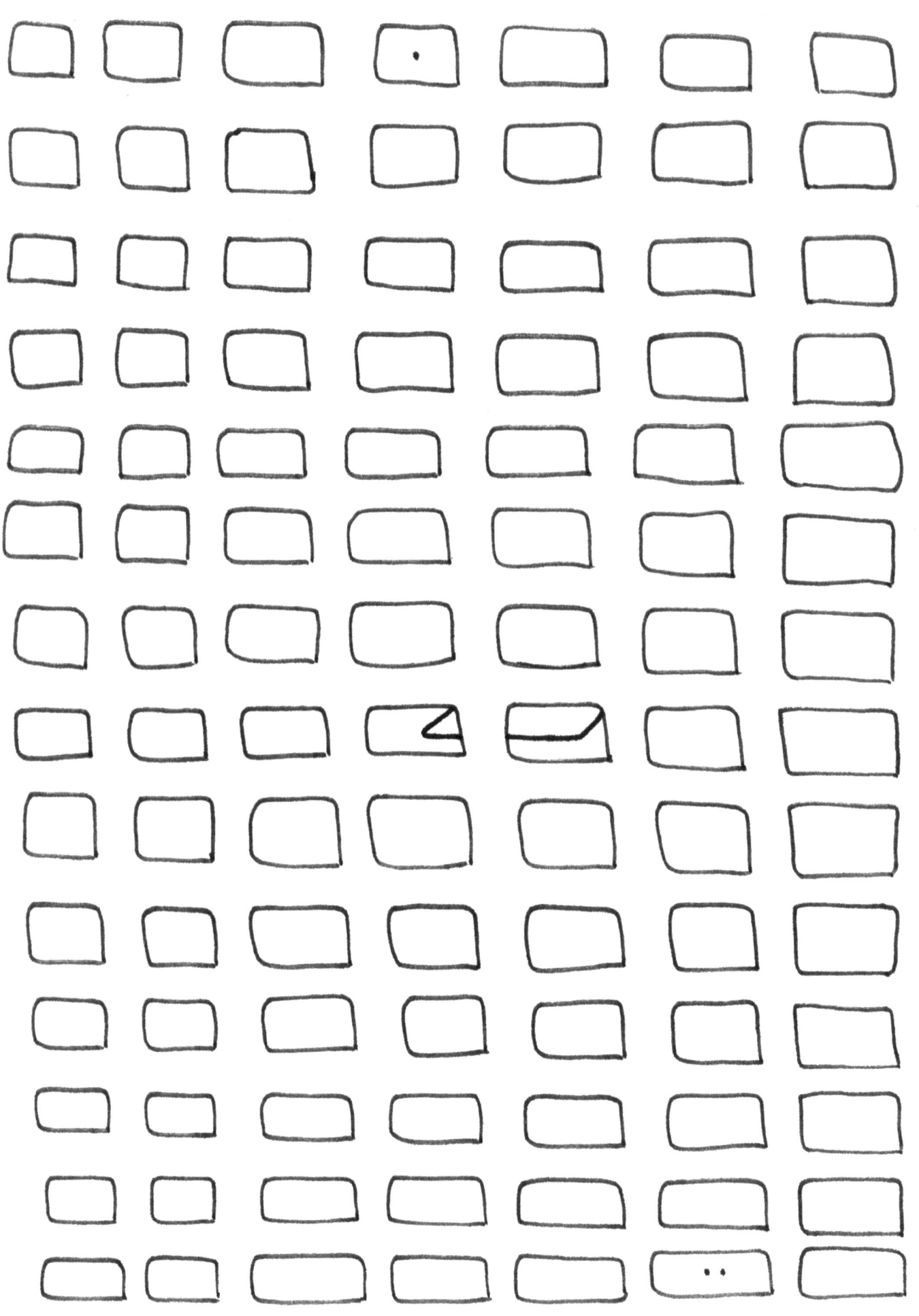

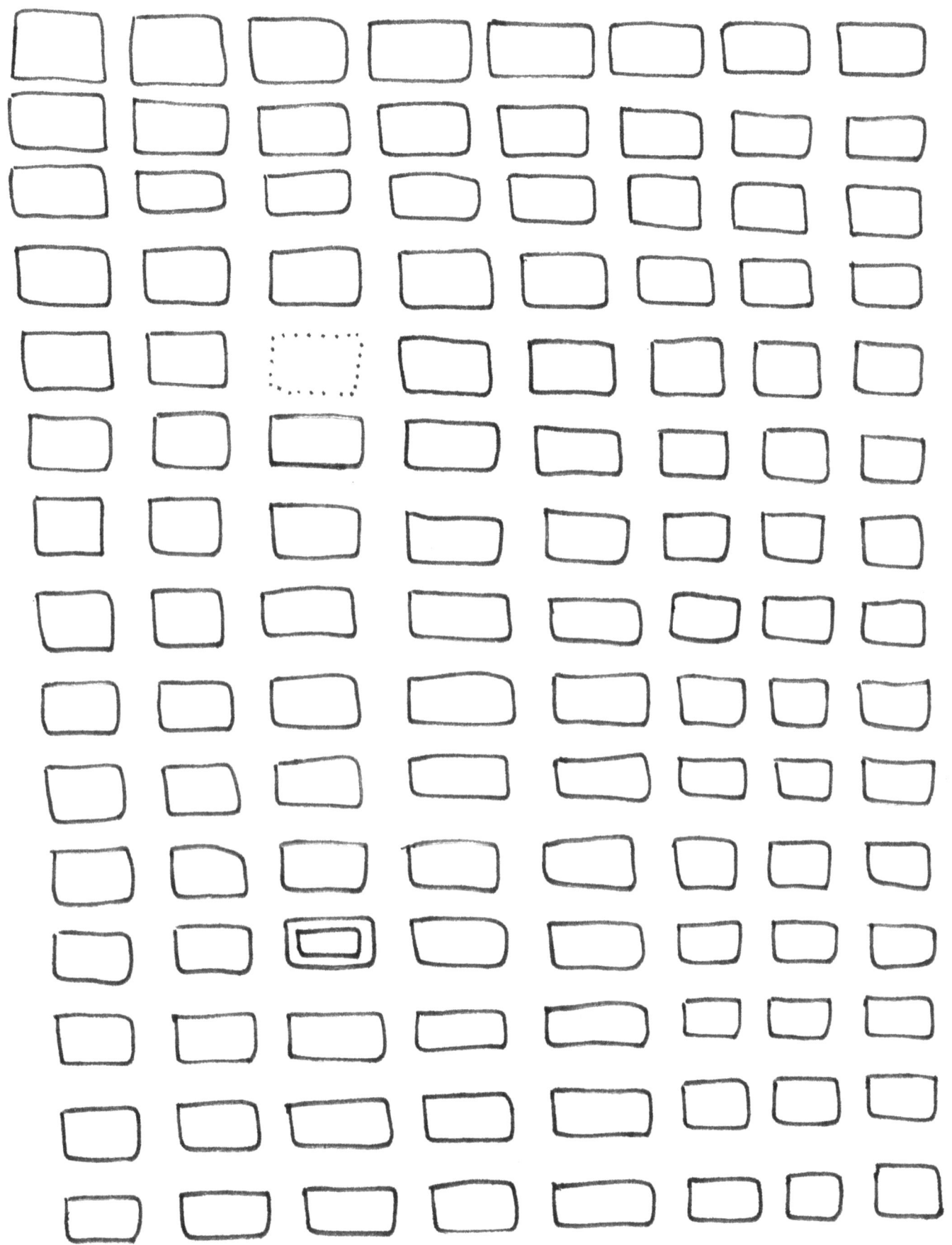

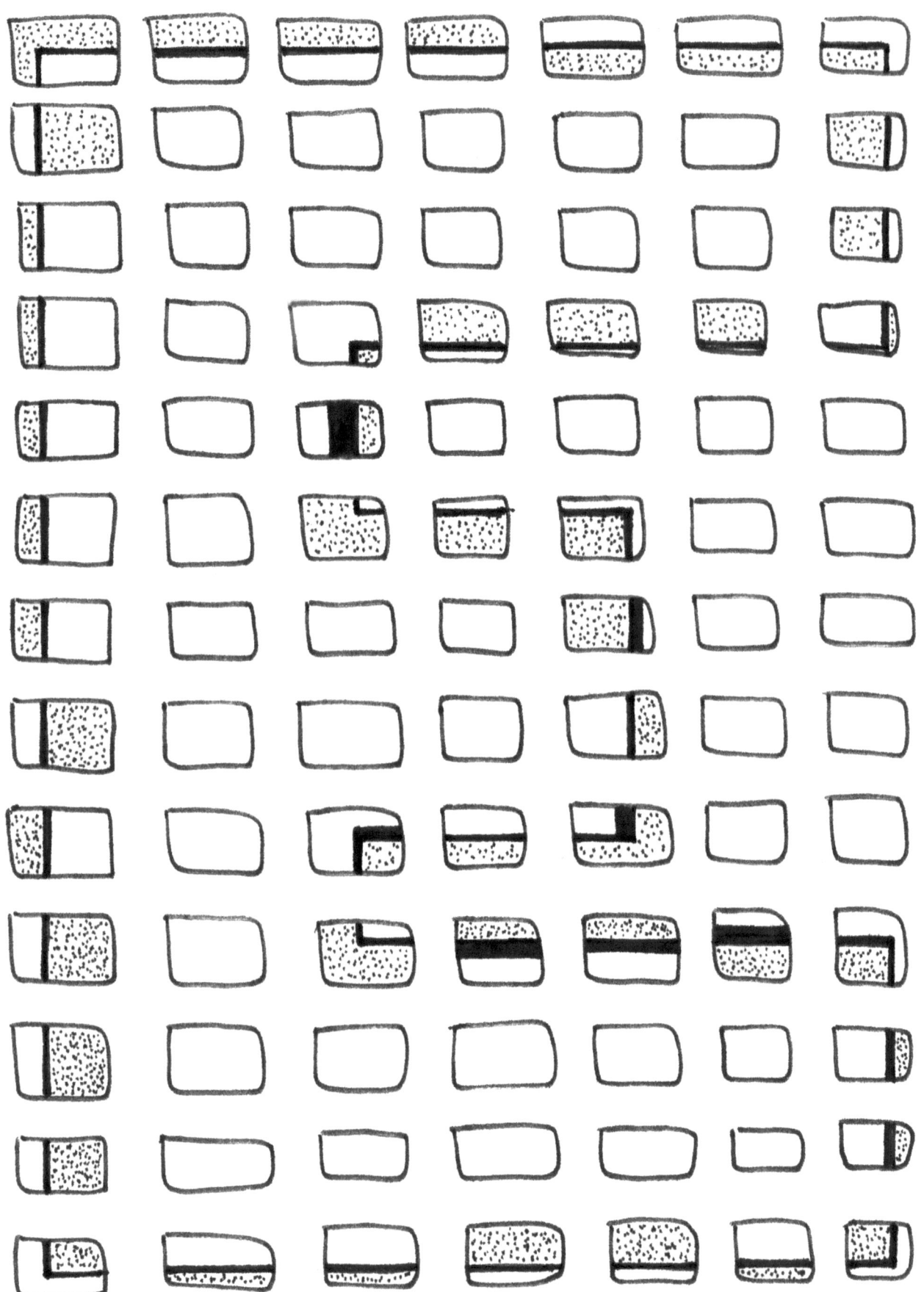

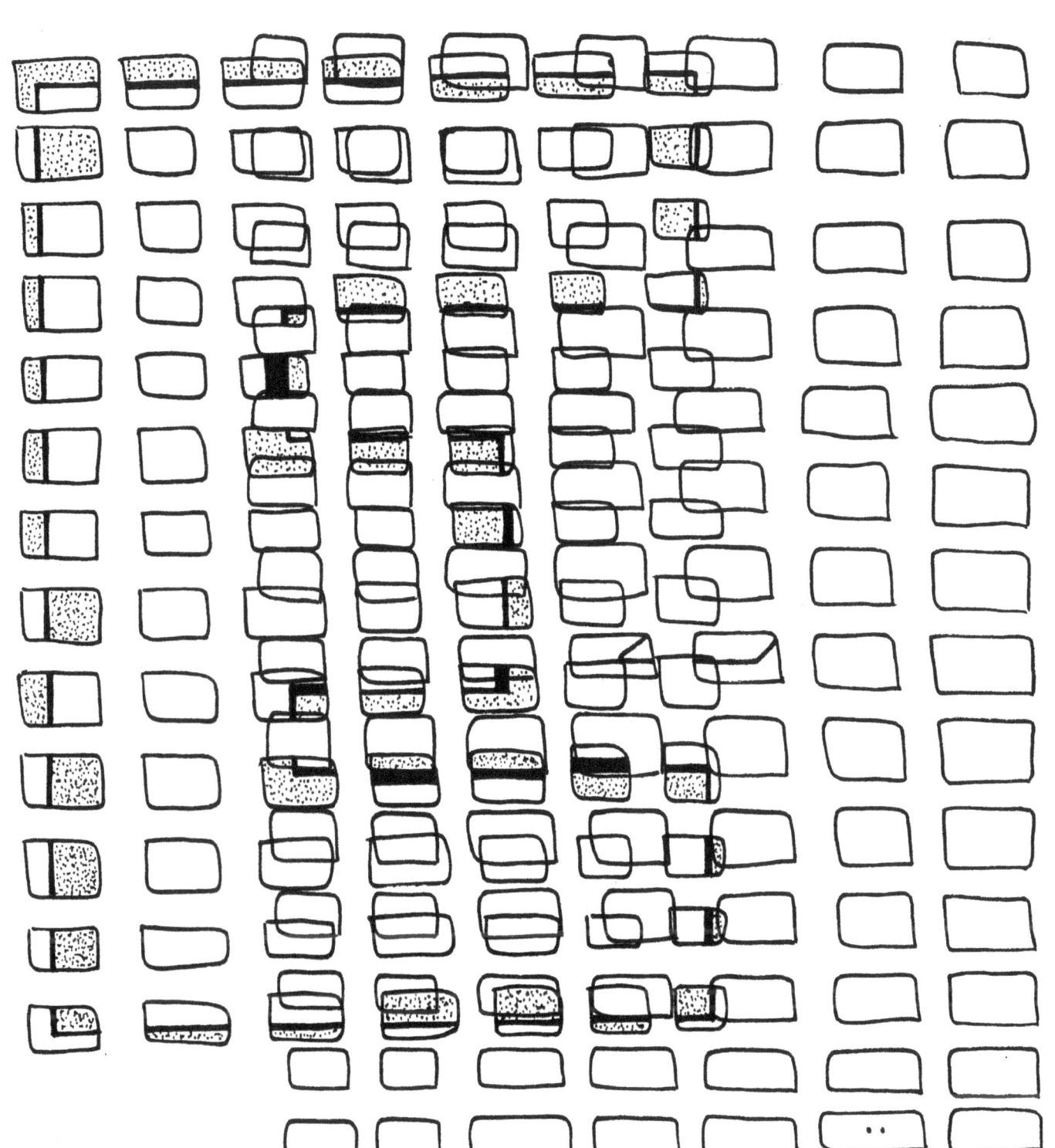

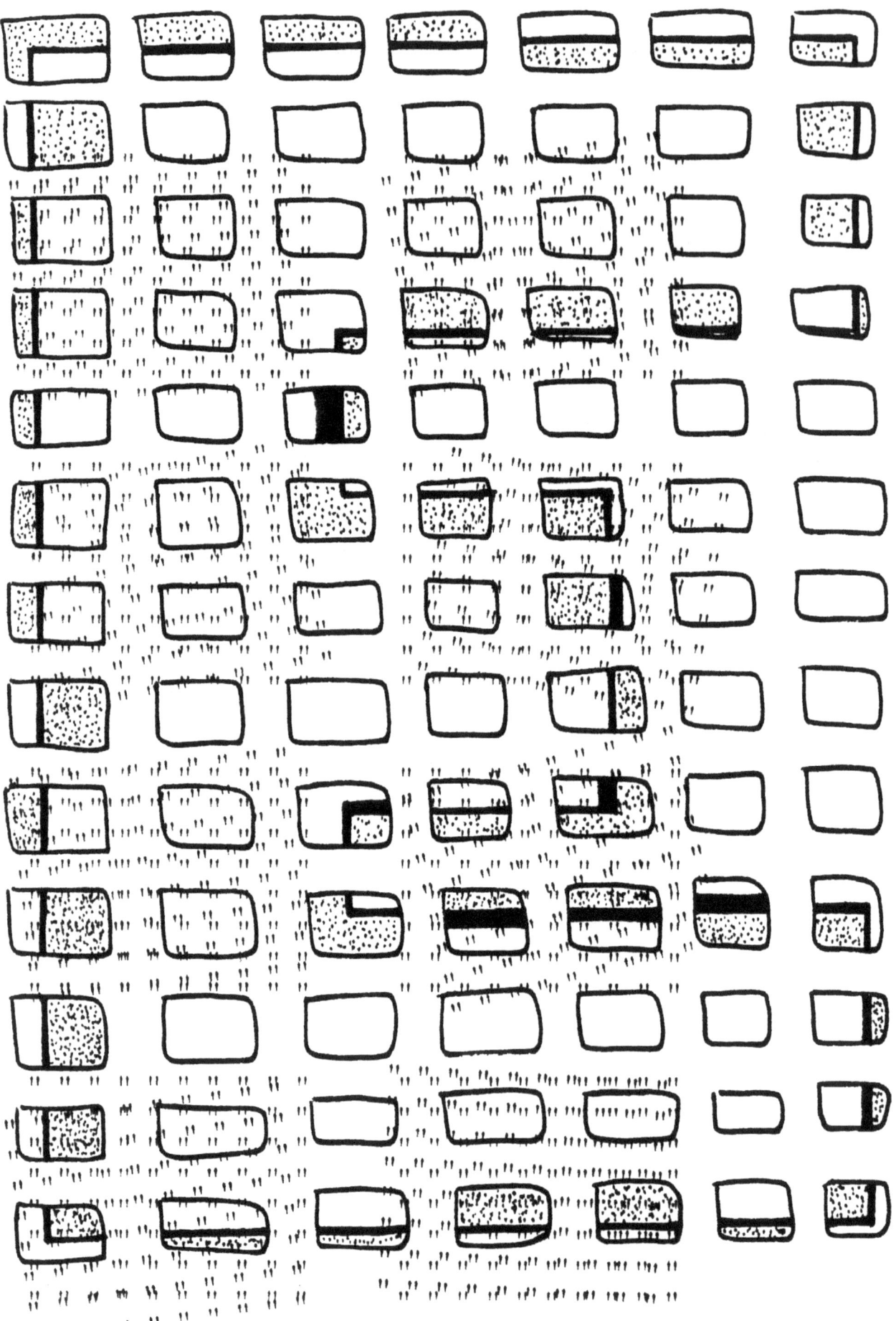

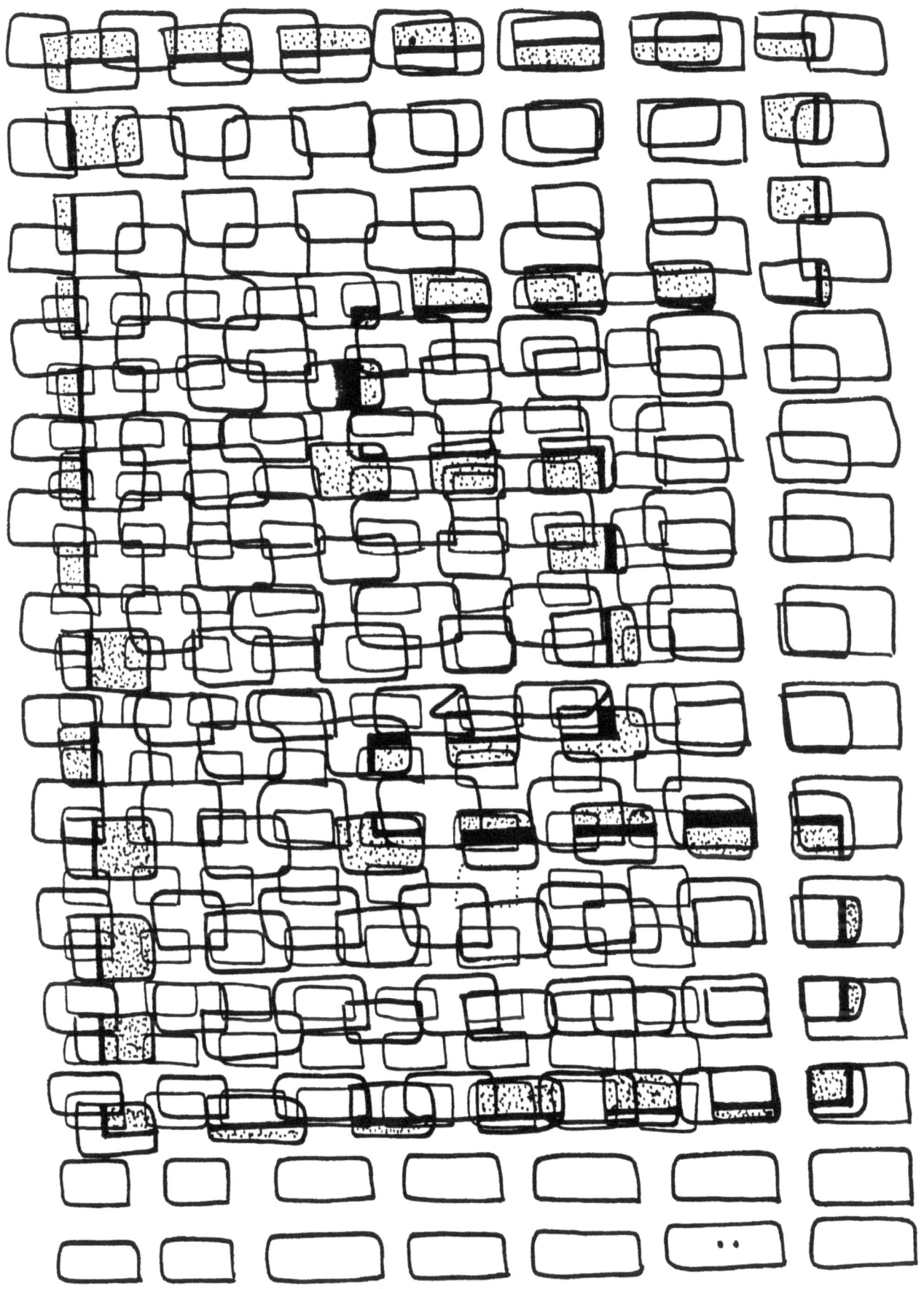

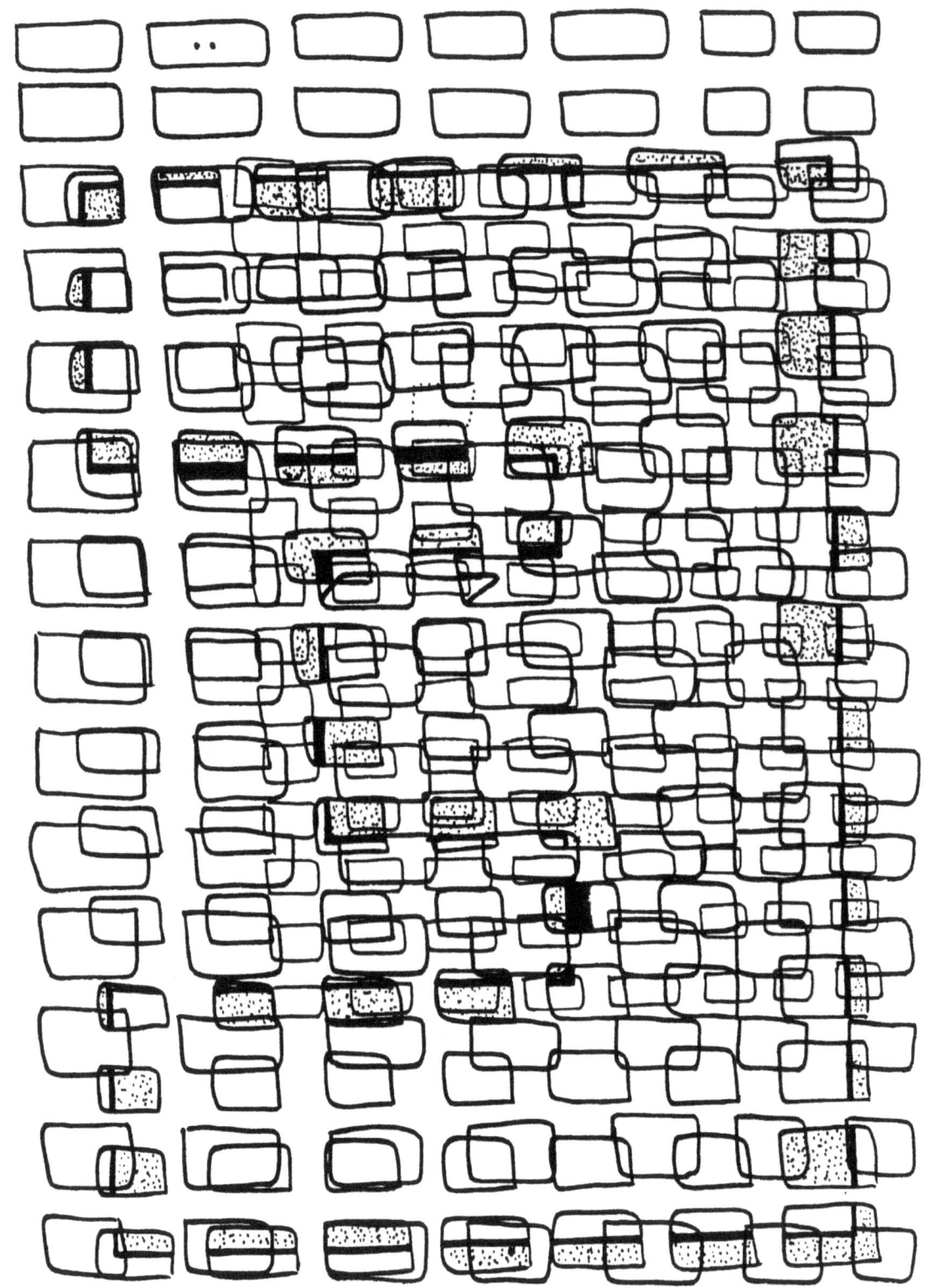

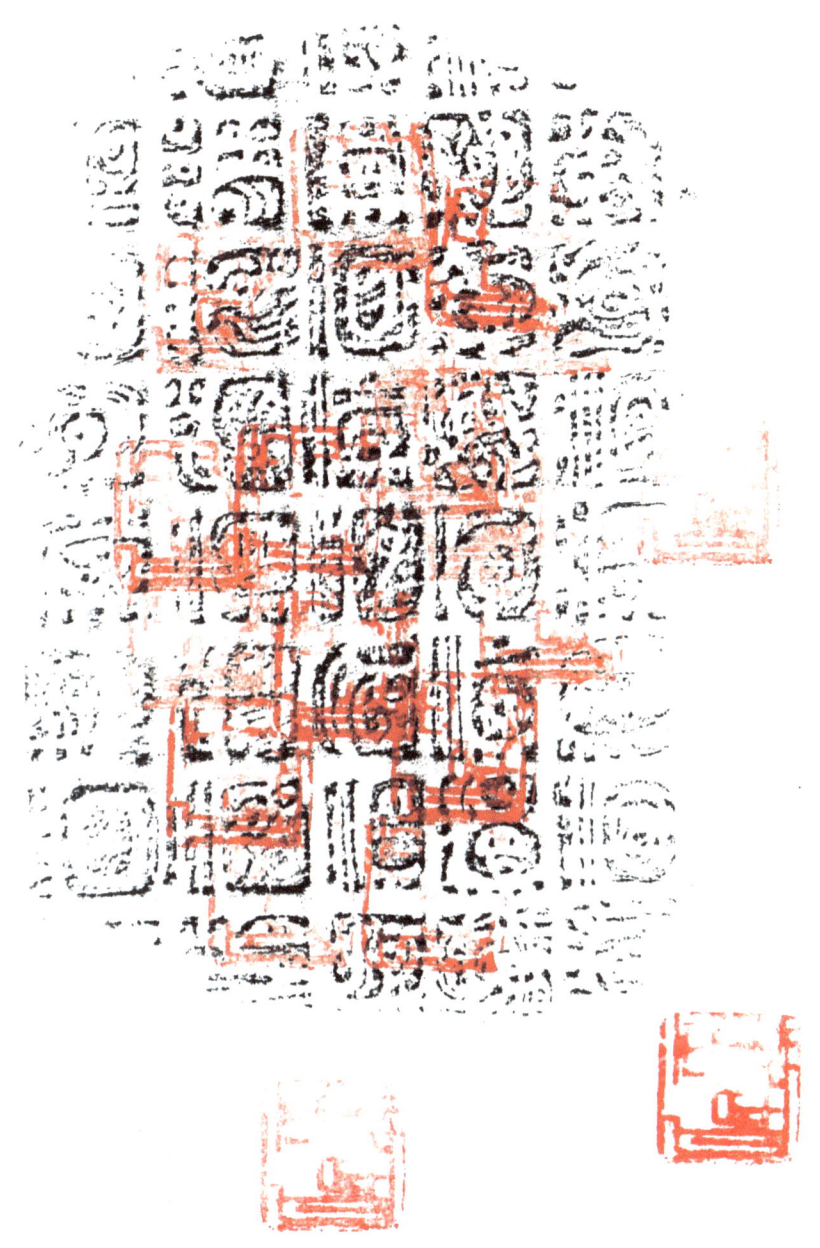

MISCELLANEOUS HOLOGRAPHS (1969-75)

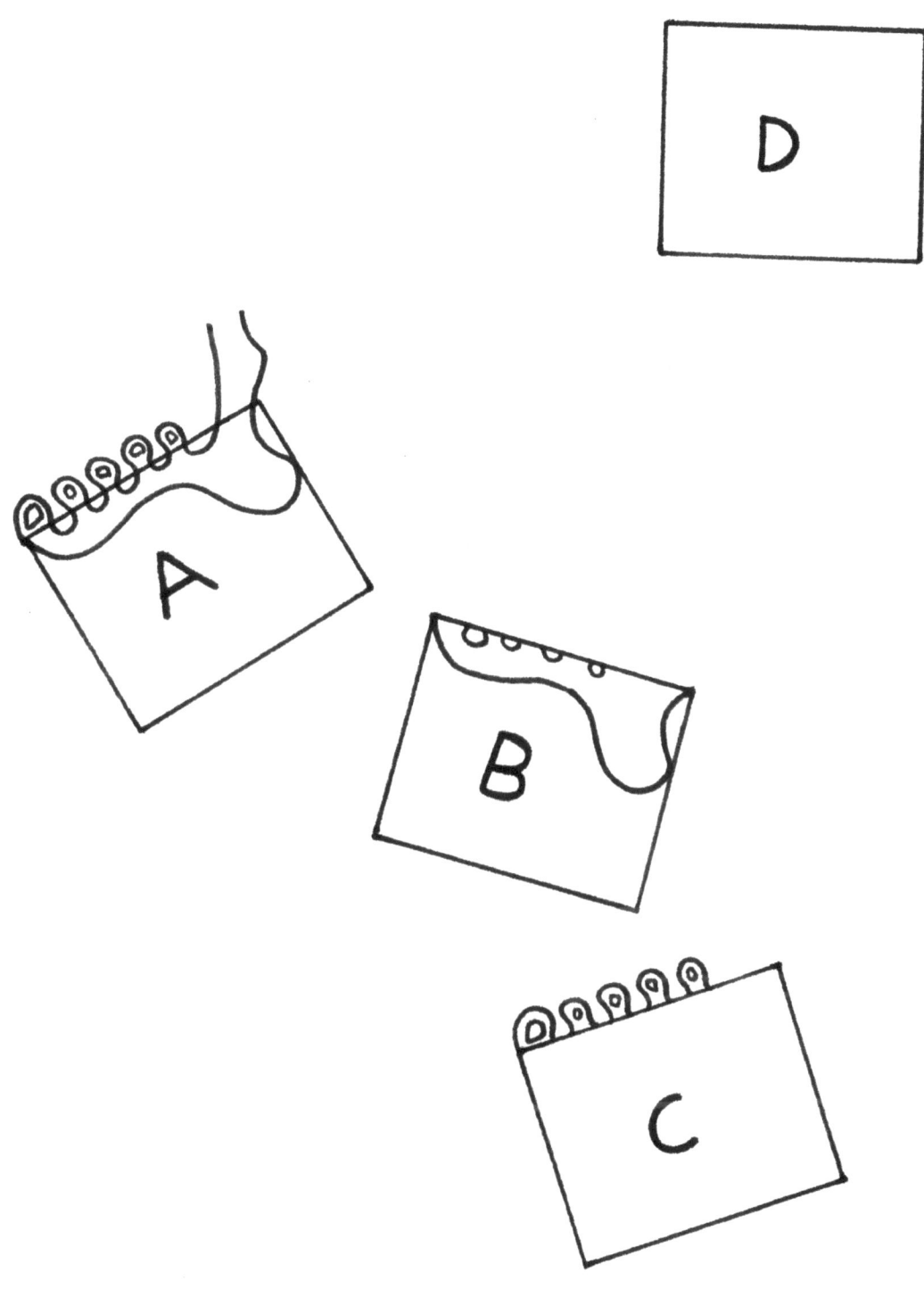

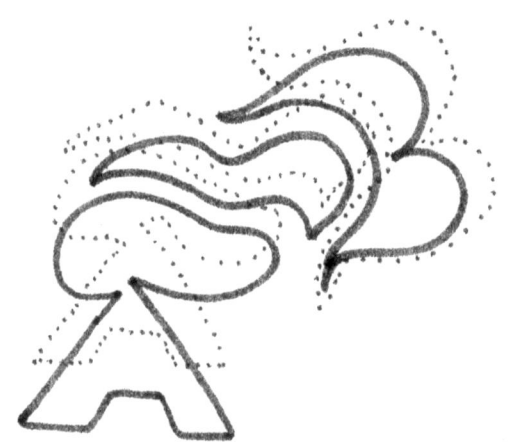

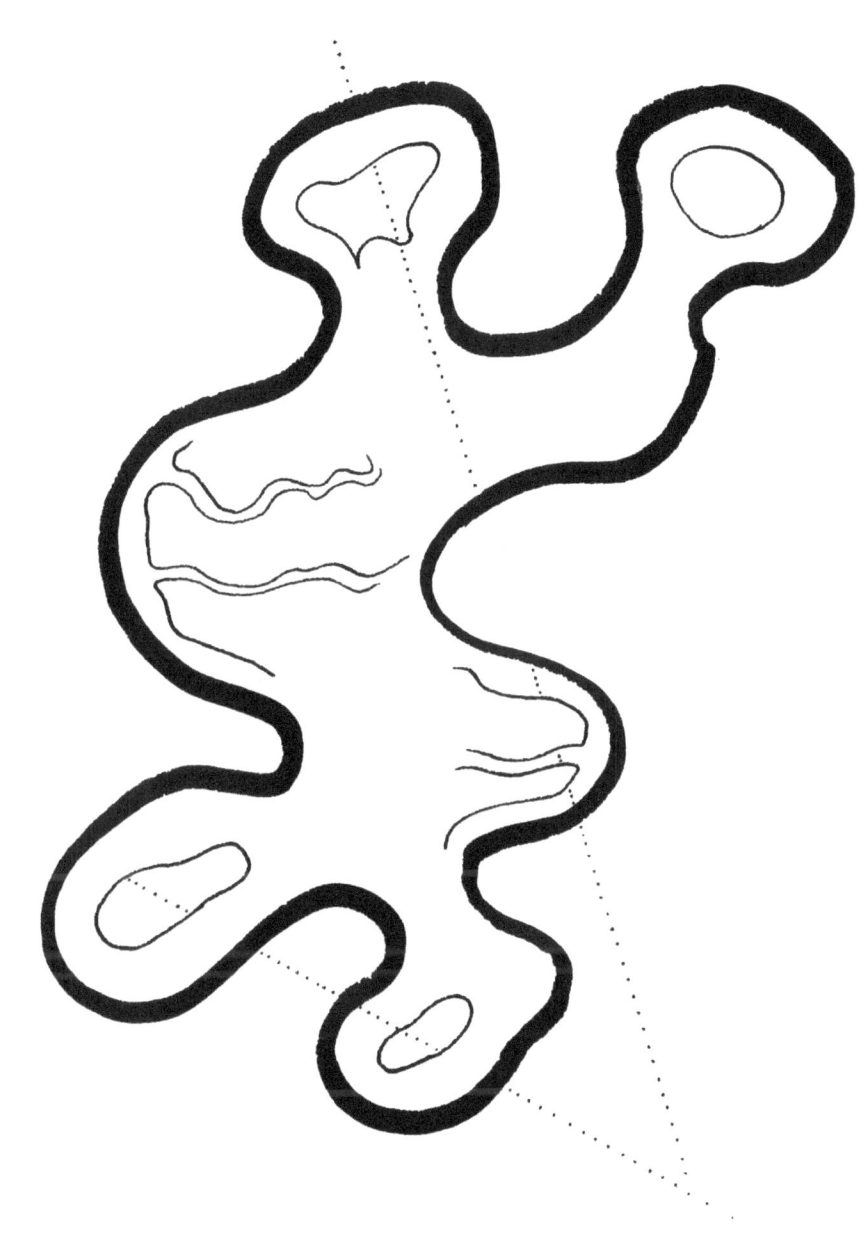

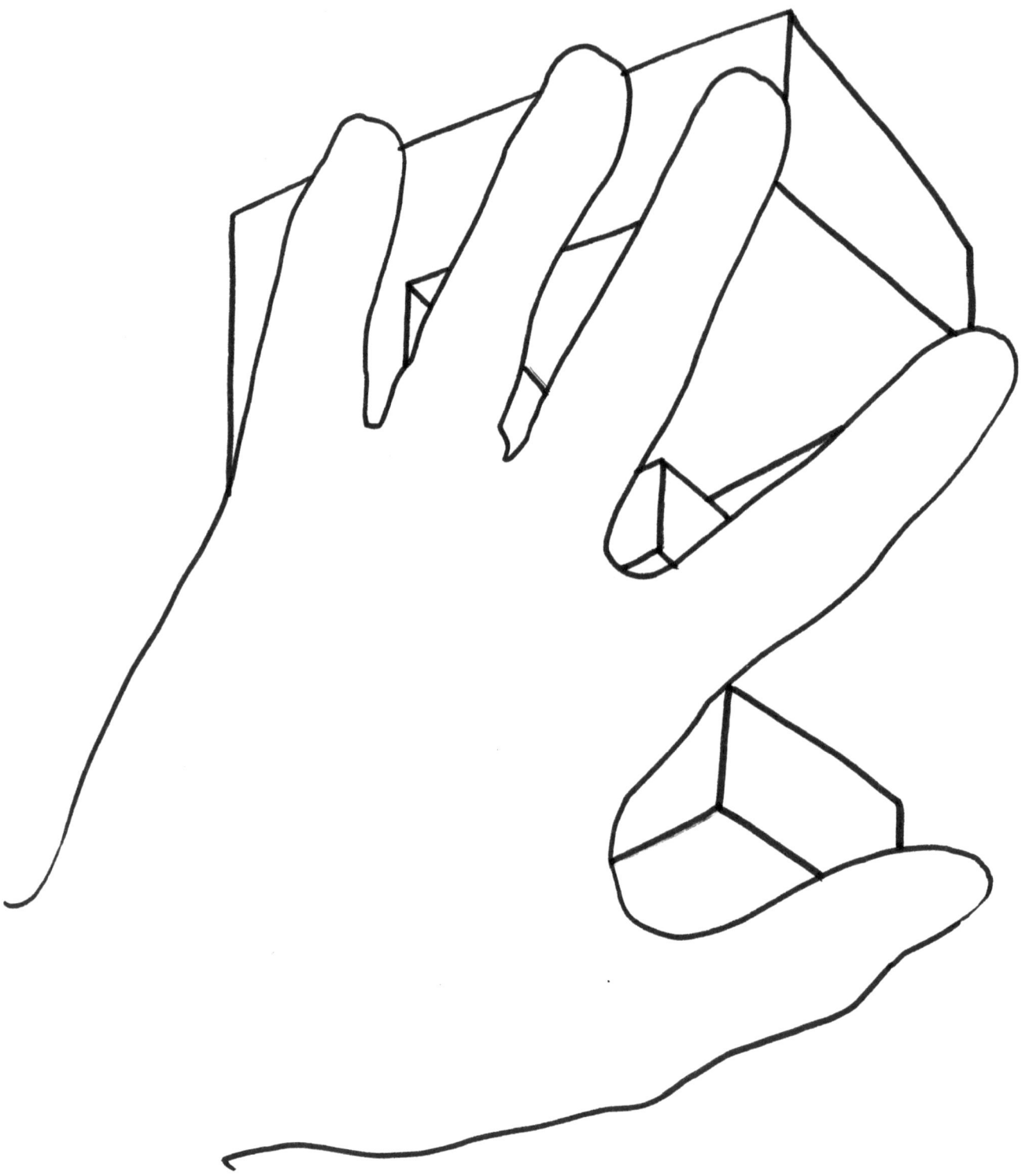

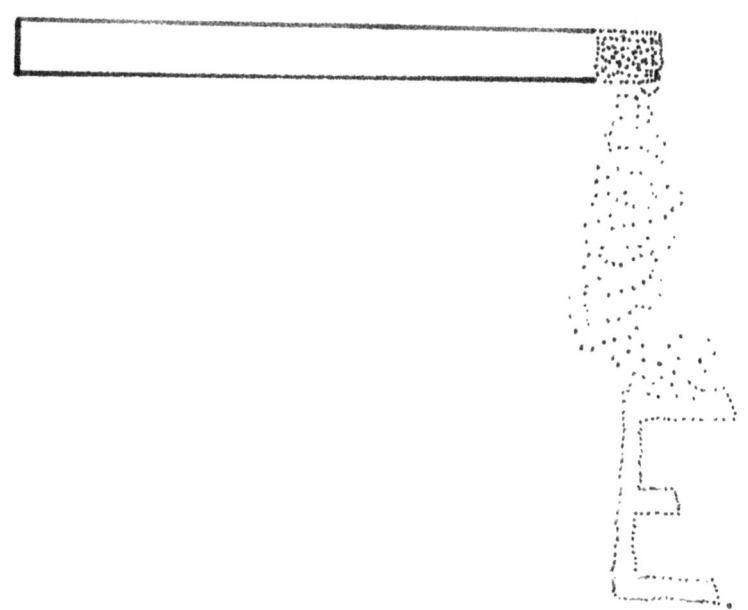

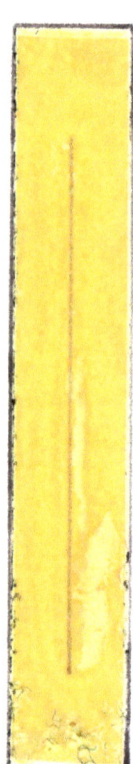 

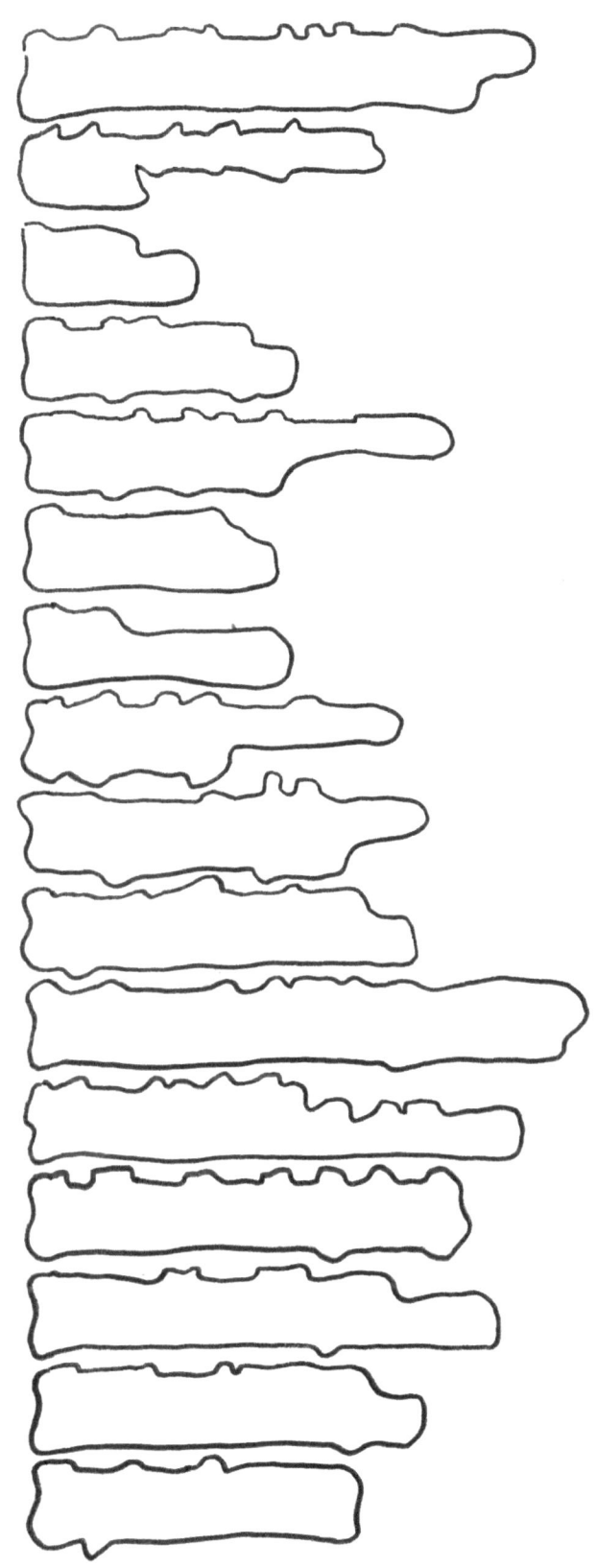

VISUAL COLLAGES (1969-85)

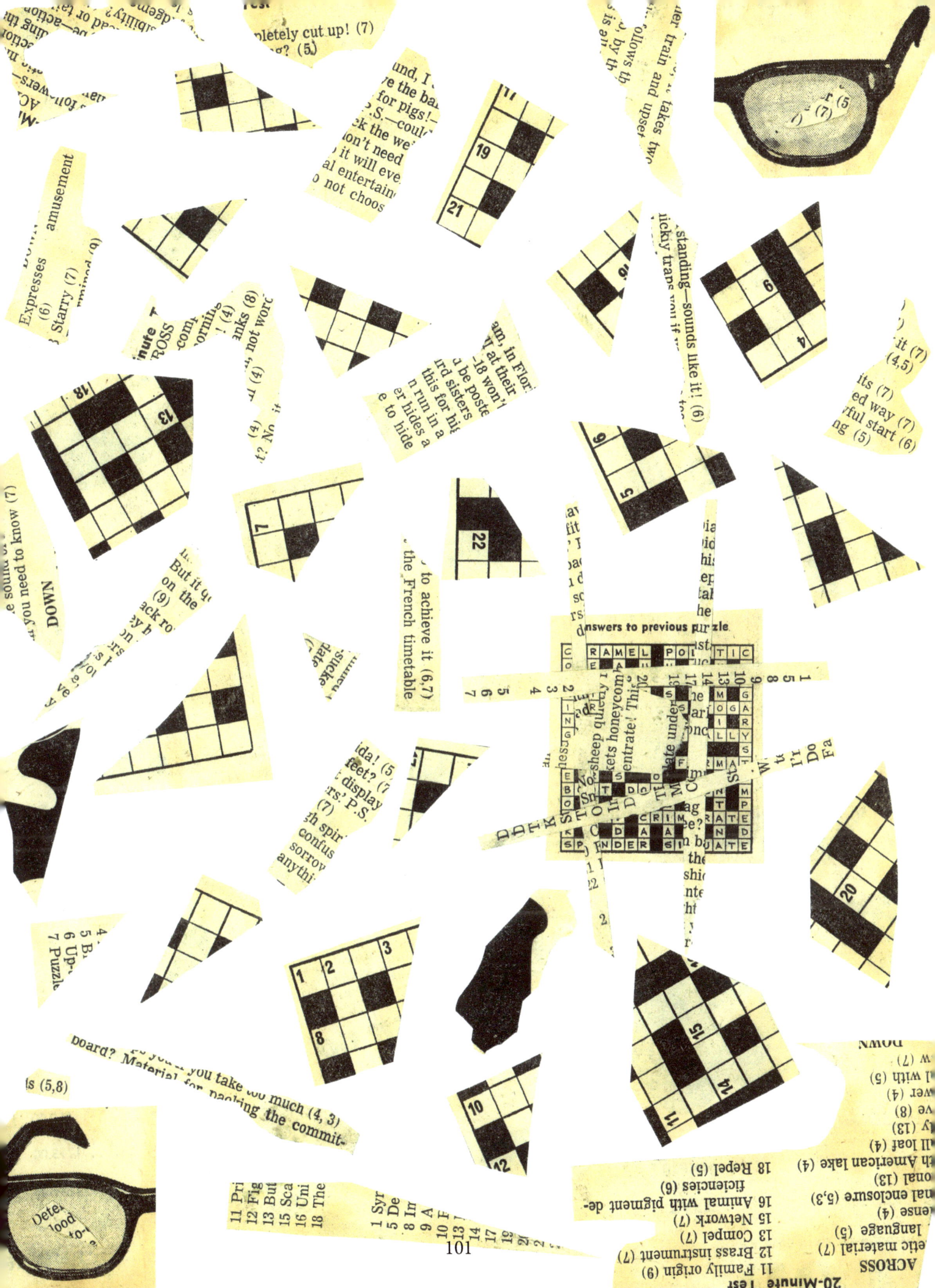

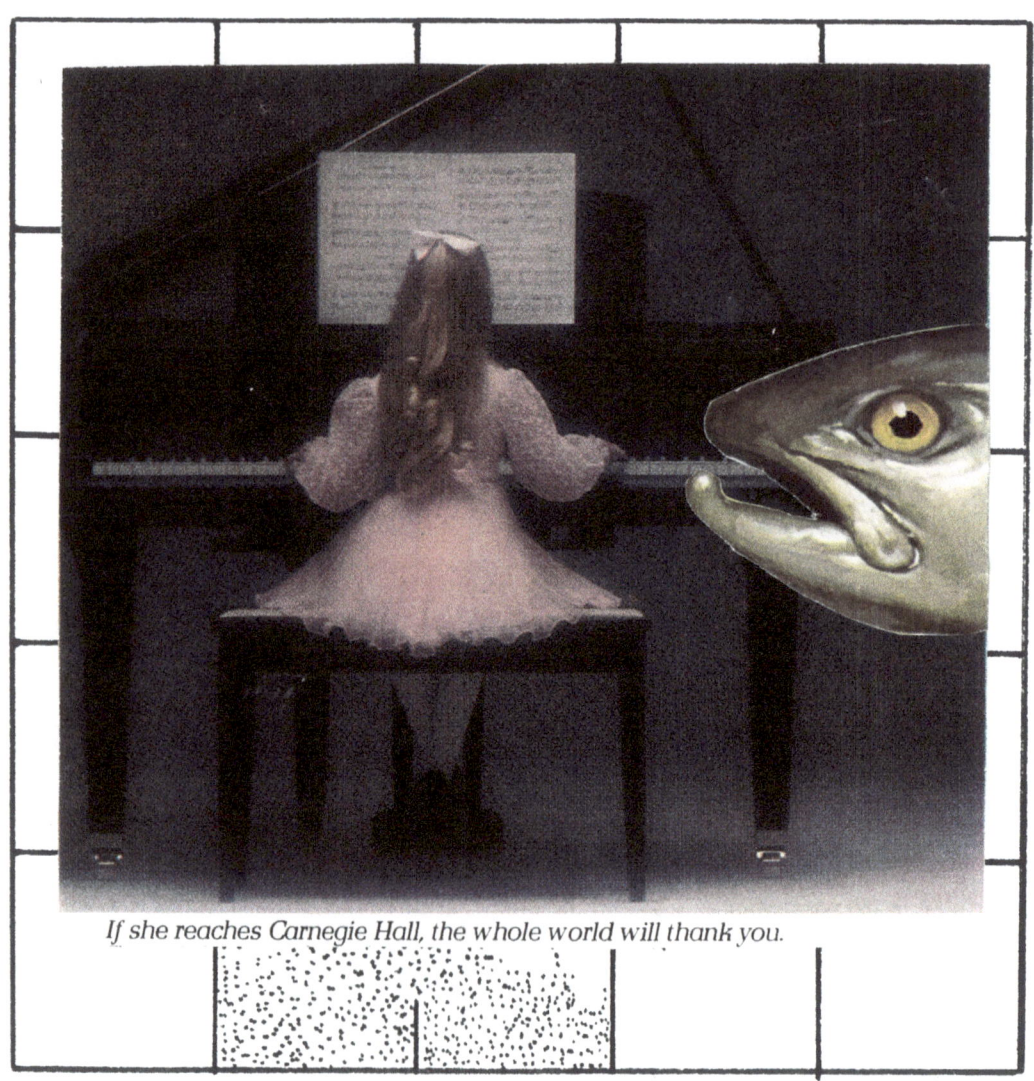

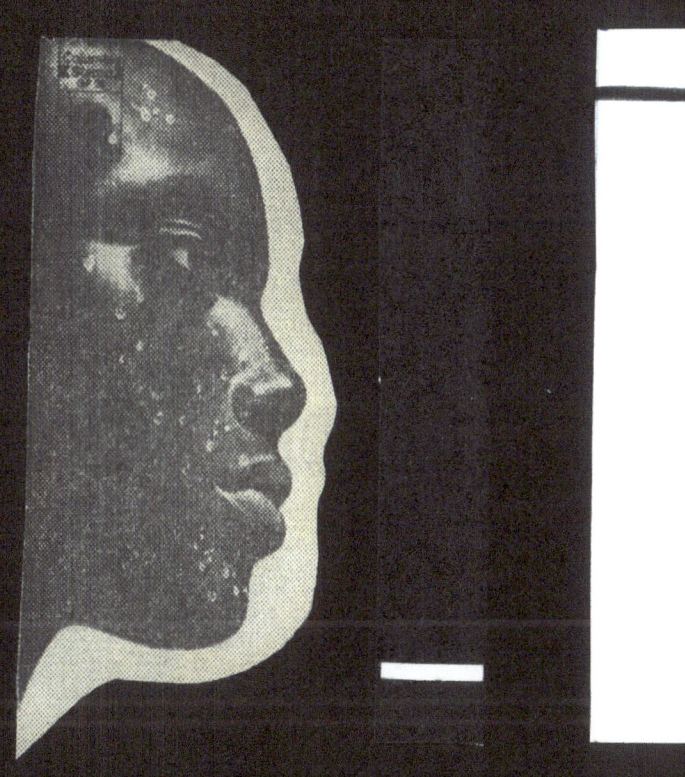

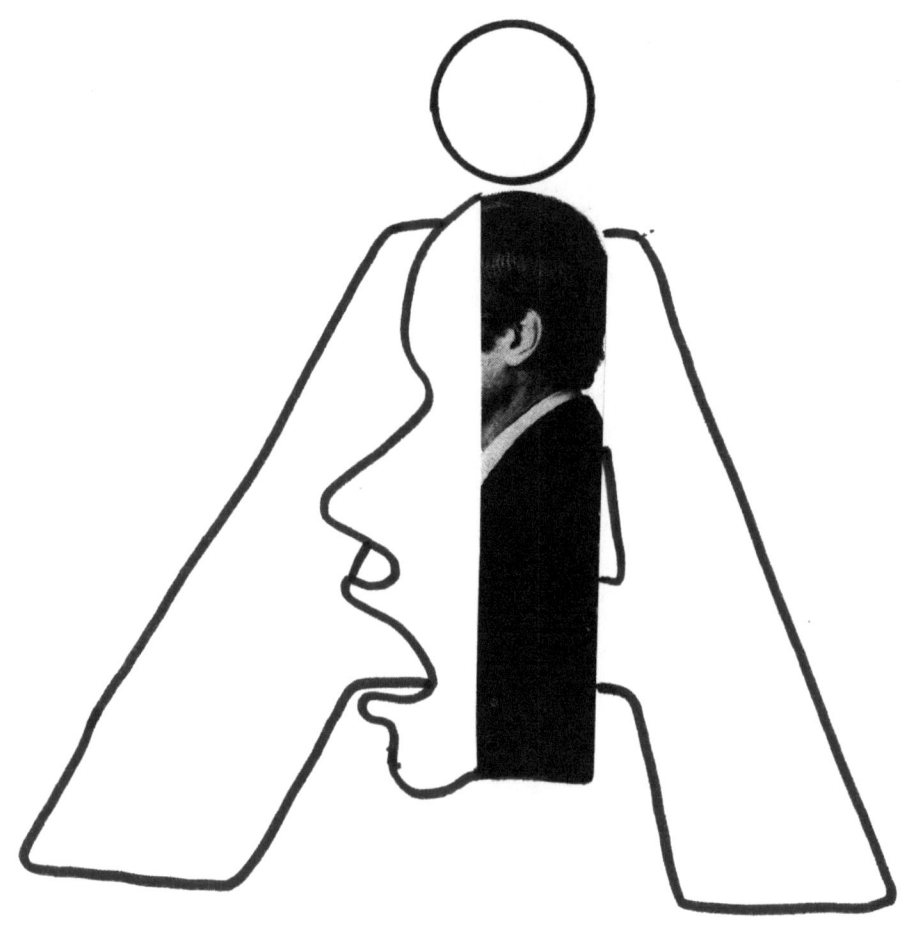

John Cage's midget parachutists
　　landing from left to right:

　　　　　　　　　　　　　Tricholoma personatum

　　　　　　　　　　　　　Coprinus micaceus

　　　　　　　　　　　　　Marasmius oreades

　　　　　　　　　　　　　Agaricus campestris

Password:
Cepes à la Bordelaise

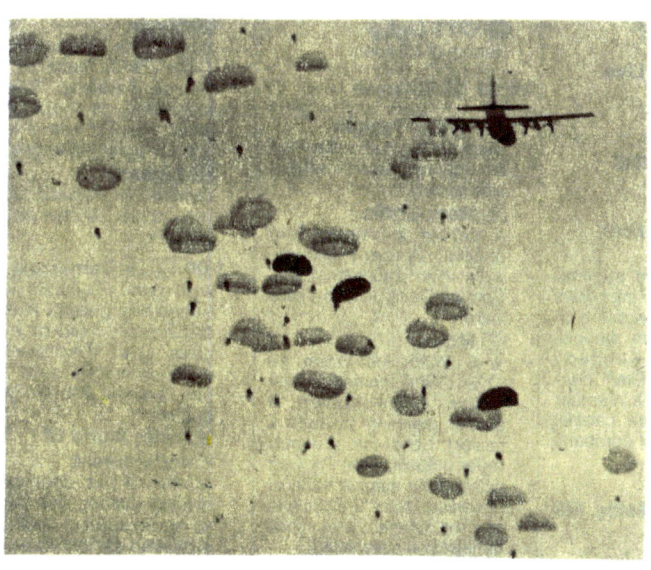

　　　　　　　　　　　　Signed: Amanita Verna.

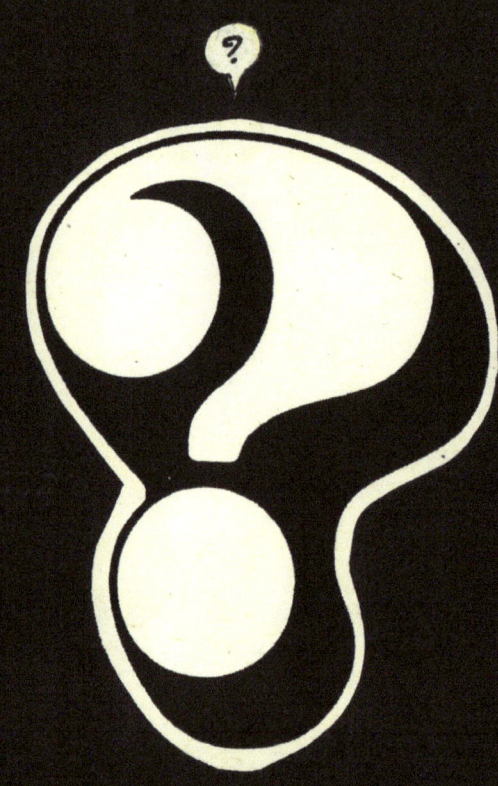

AGAINST WRITING [ASEMIC TEXTS]
(1972-85)

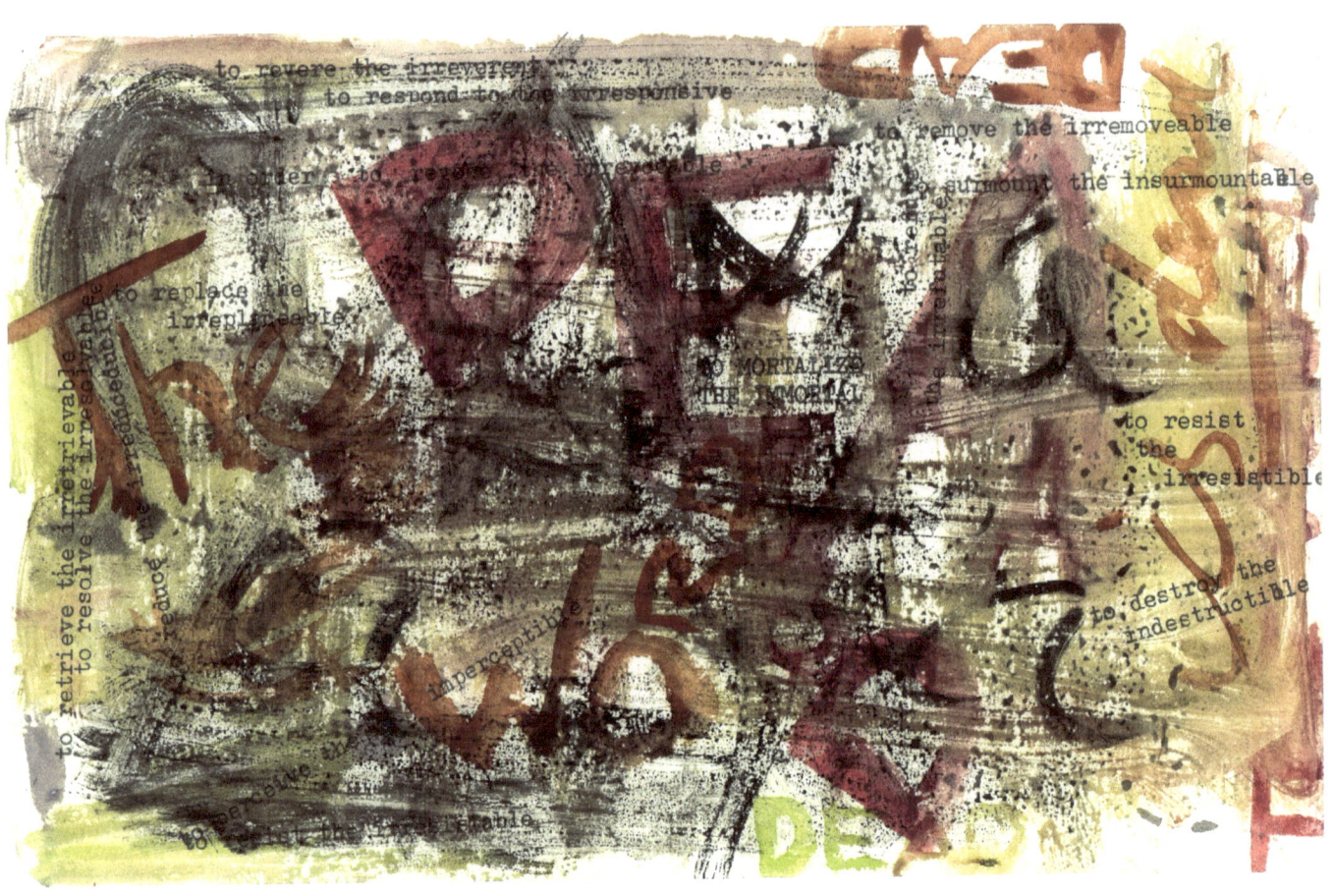

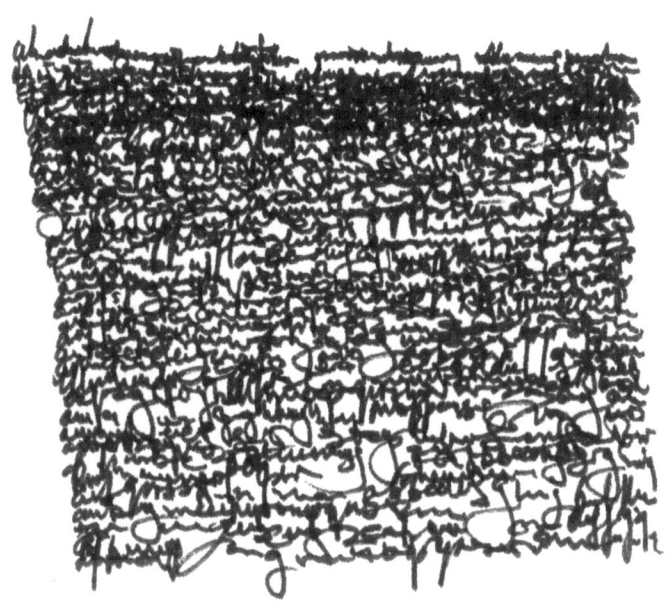

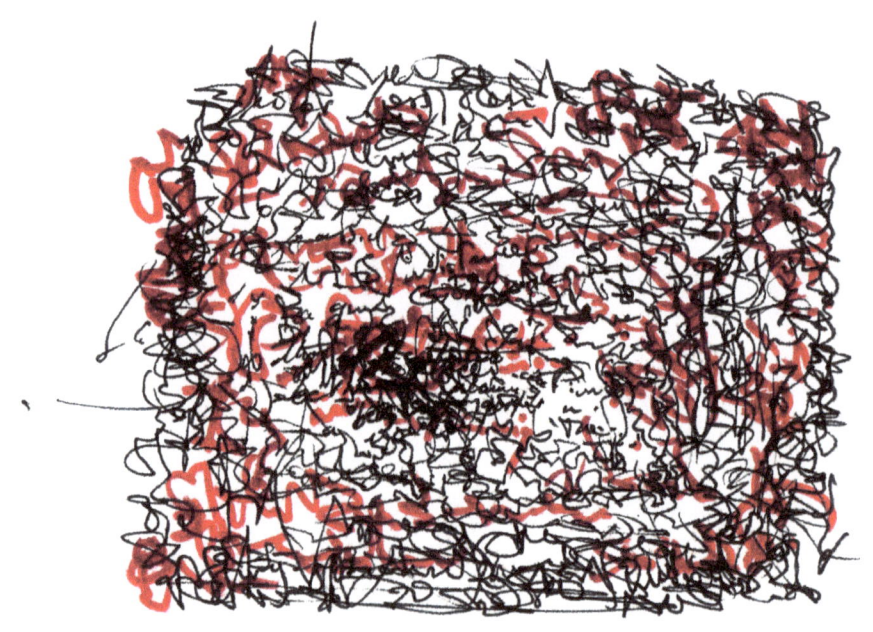

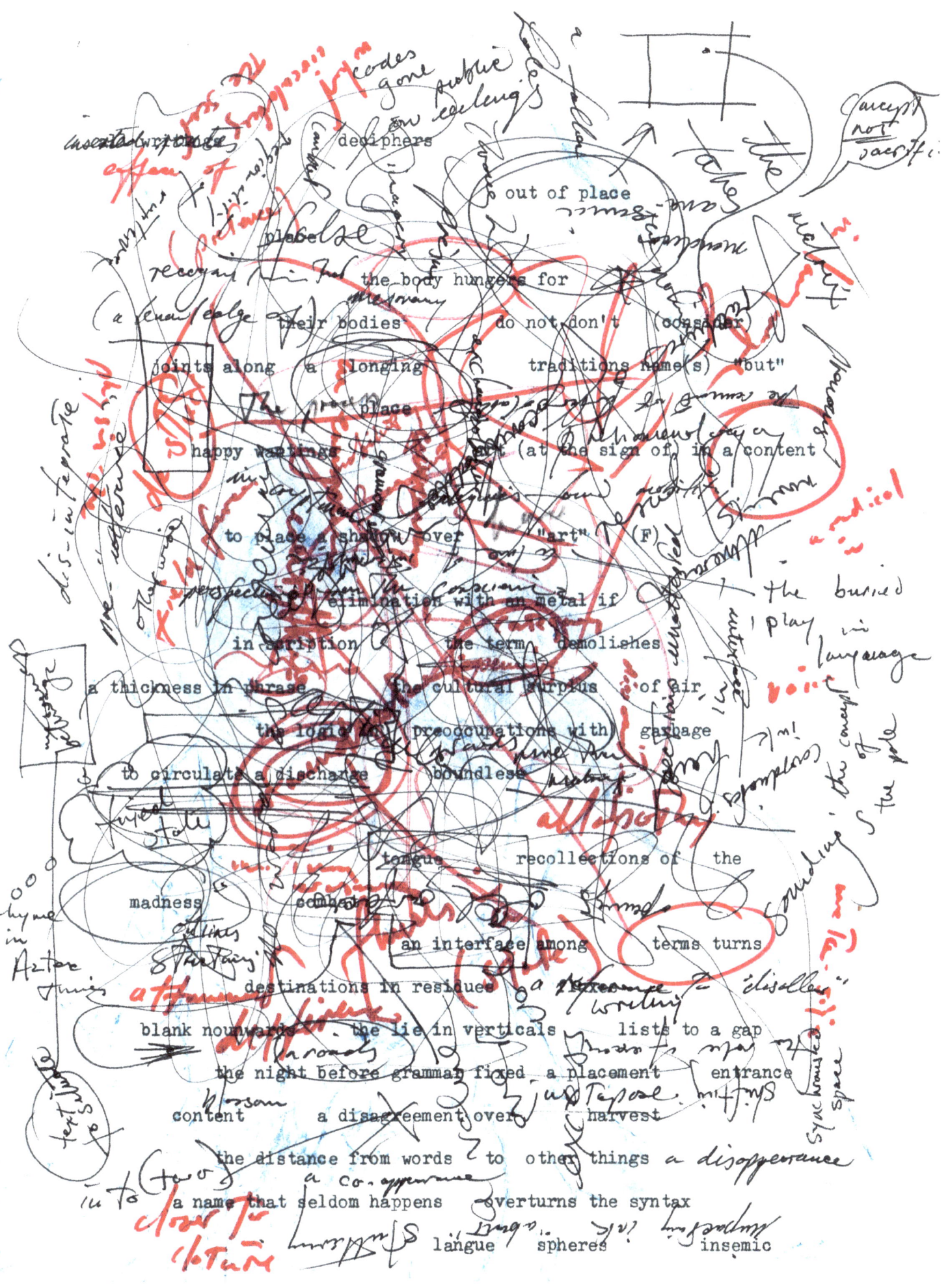

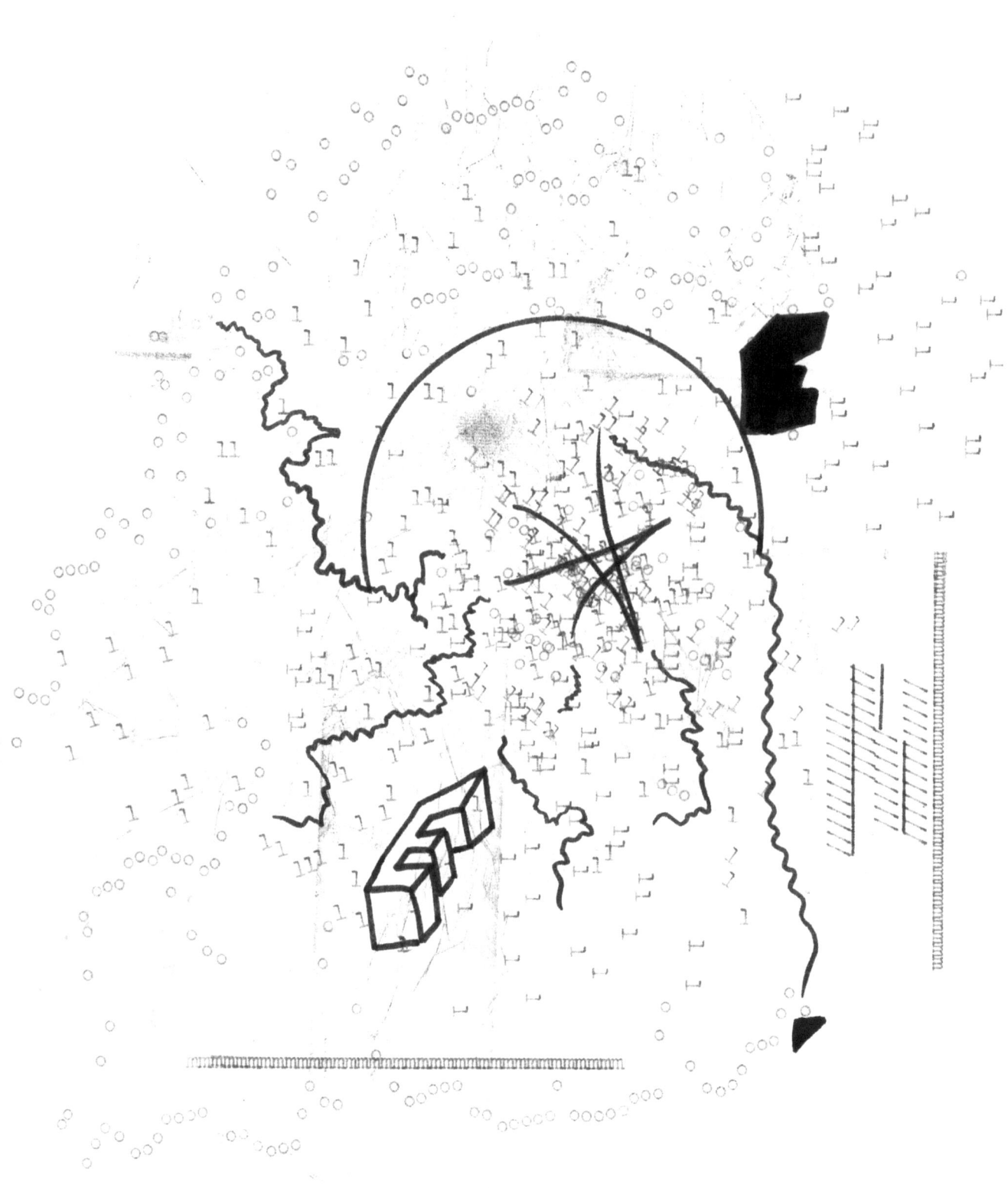

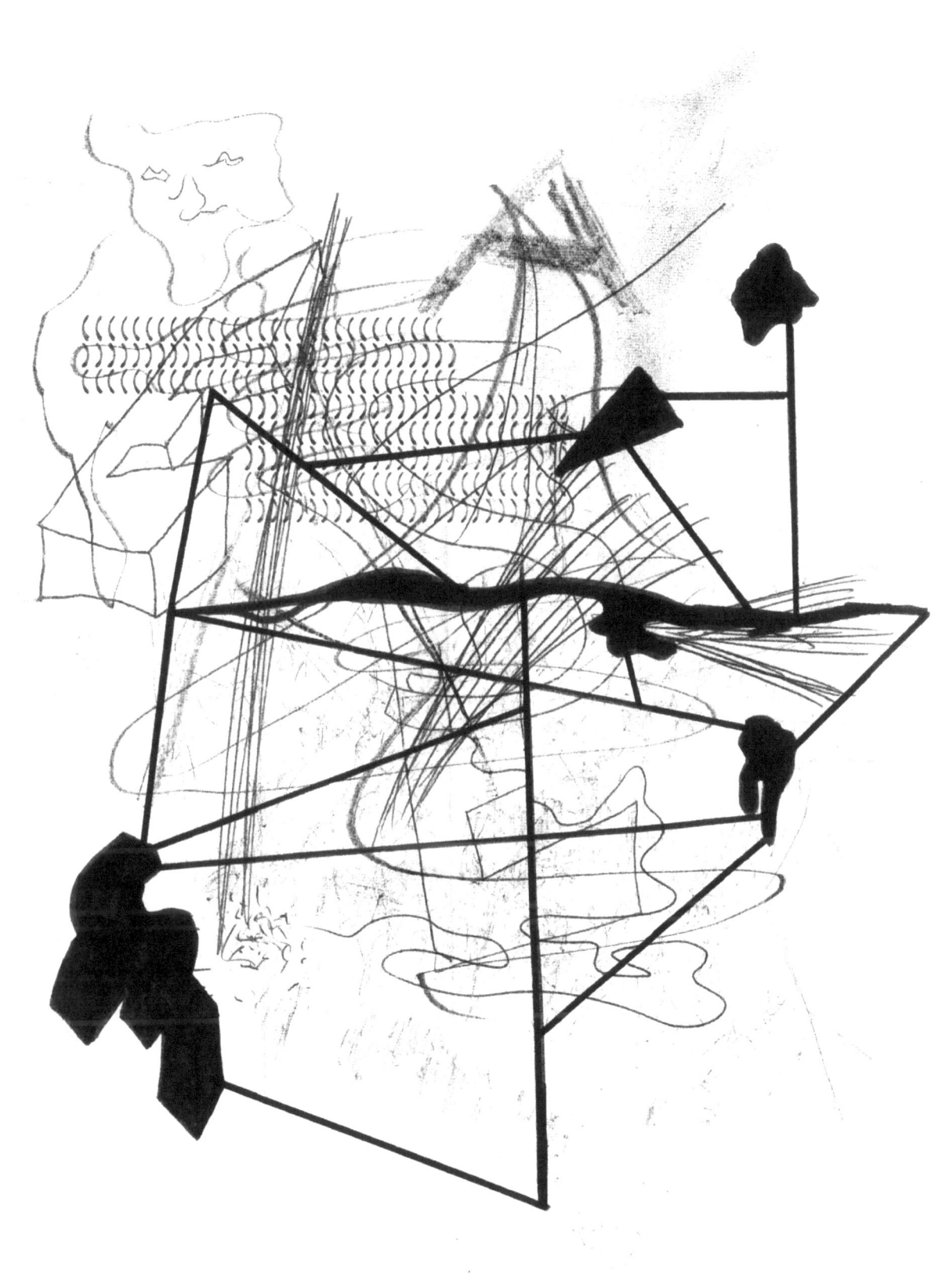

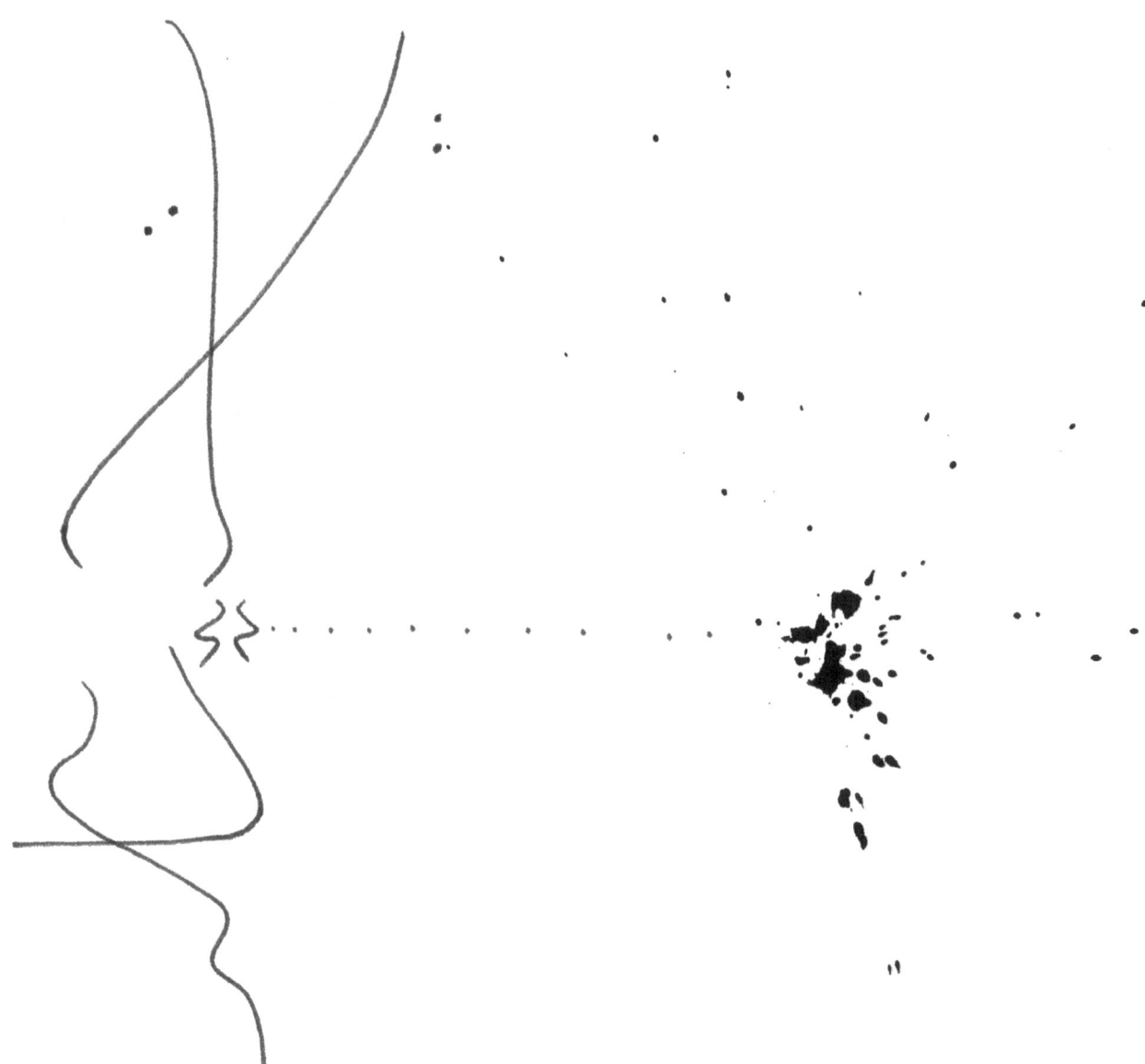

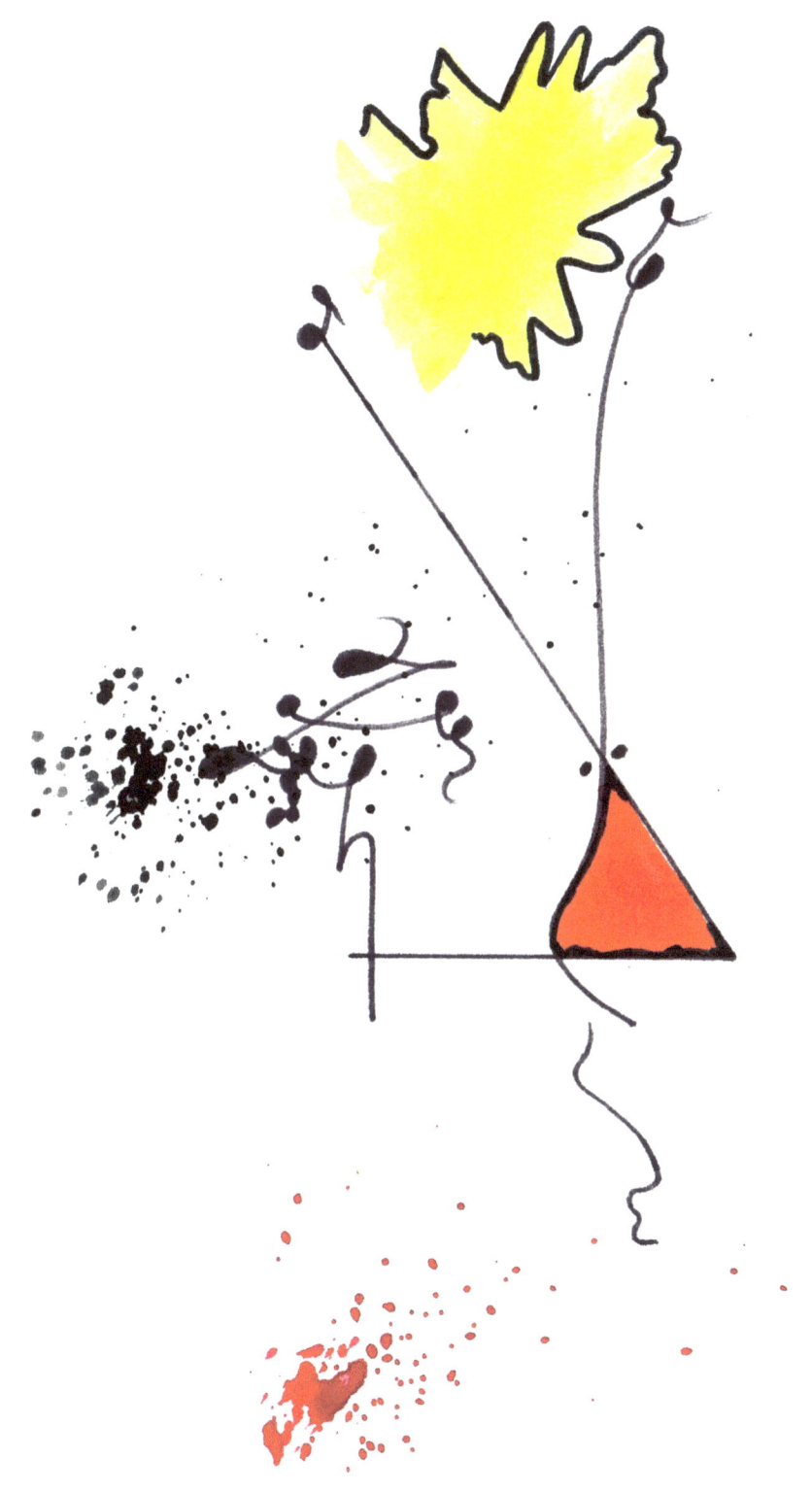

SIX VISUAL POEMS (2009)

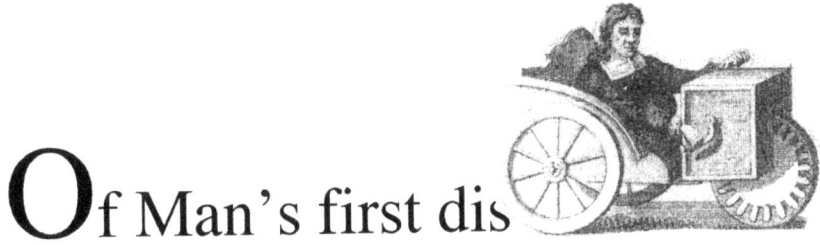

Of Man's first dis

Milton enters the left foot of Marinetti to start his grand epic

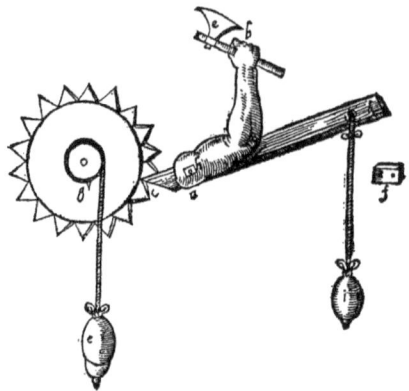

Ephebic Consequences of the iambic pentameter

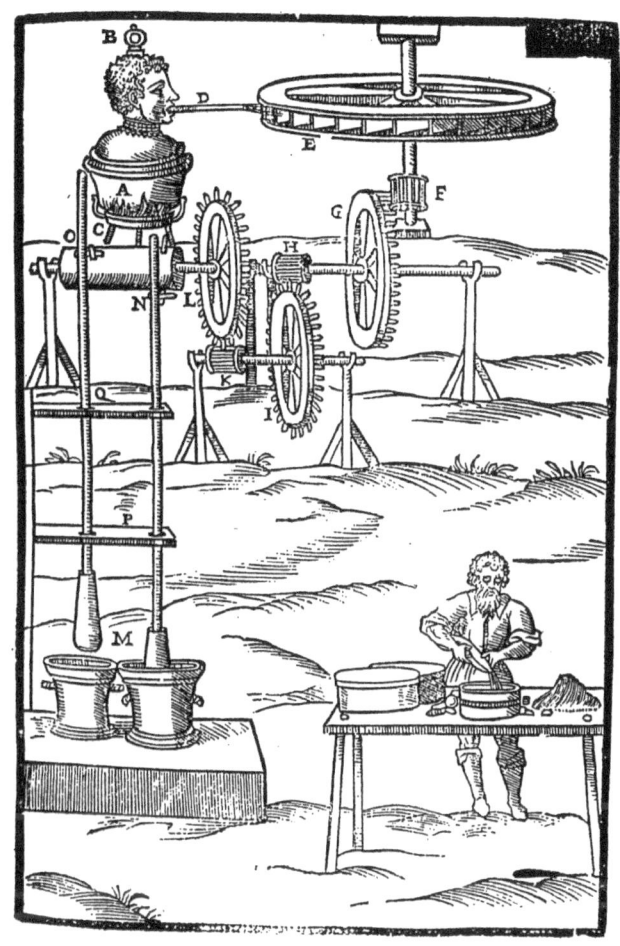

Projective Verse 1
"A poem is energy transferred from where the poet got it
(he will have several causations), by way of the poem itself to,
all the way over to, the reader."

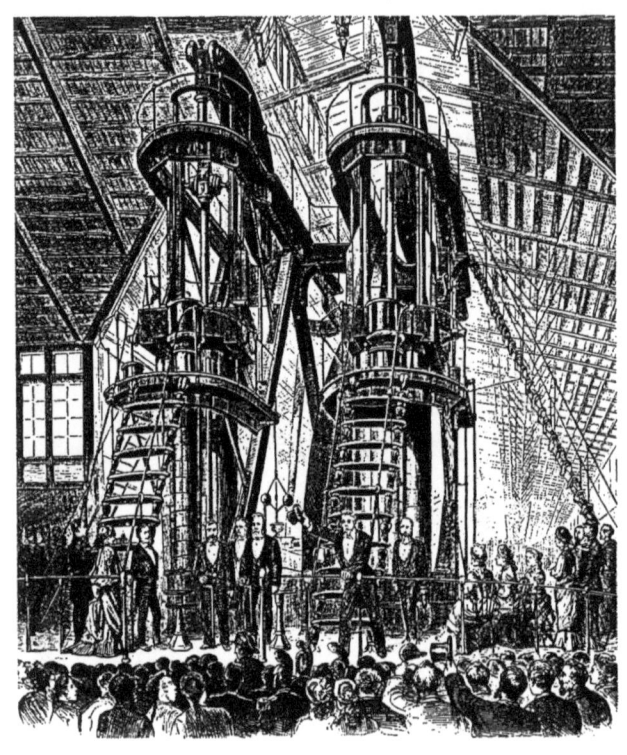

Projective Verse 2
"Then the poem itself must, at all points, be a high energy-construct and, at all points, an energy-discharge."

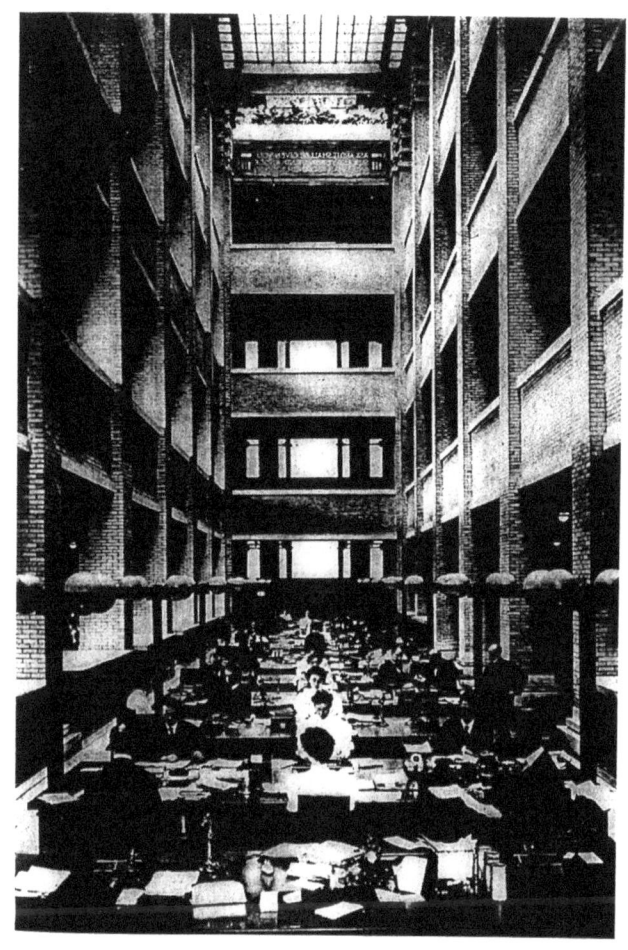

Projective Verse 3
"It is the advantage of the typewriter that, due to its rigidity and space precisions, it can, for a poet, indicate exactly the breath, the pauses, the suspensions even of syllables, . . ."
    First annual Projective Verse Convention, Columbus, Ohio.

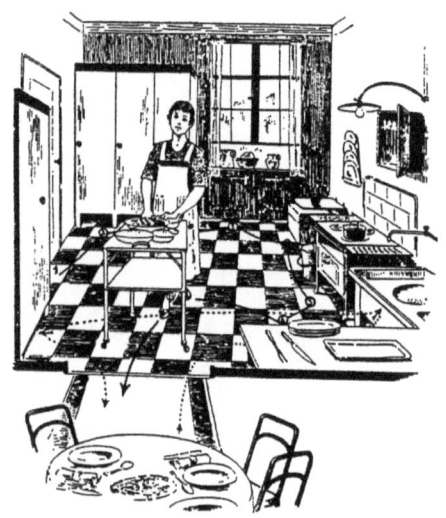

Visual Sonnet: Queen to Bishop's 1 Check!
(Mechanism of the second chess player of Leonardo Toros Queverdo, 1920)

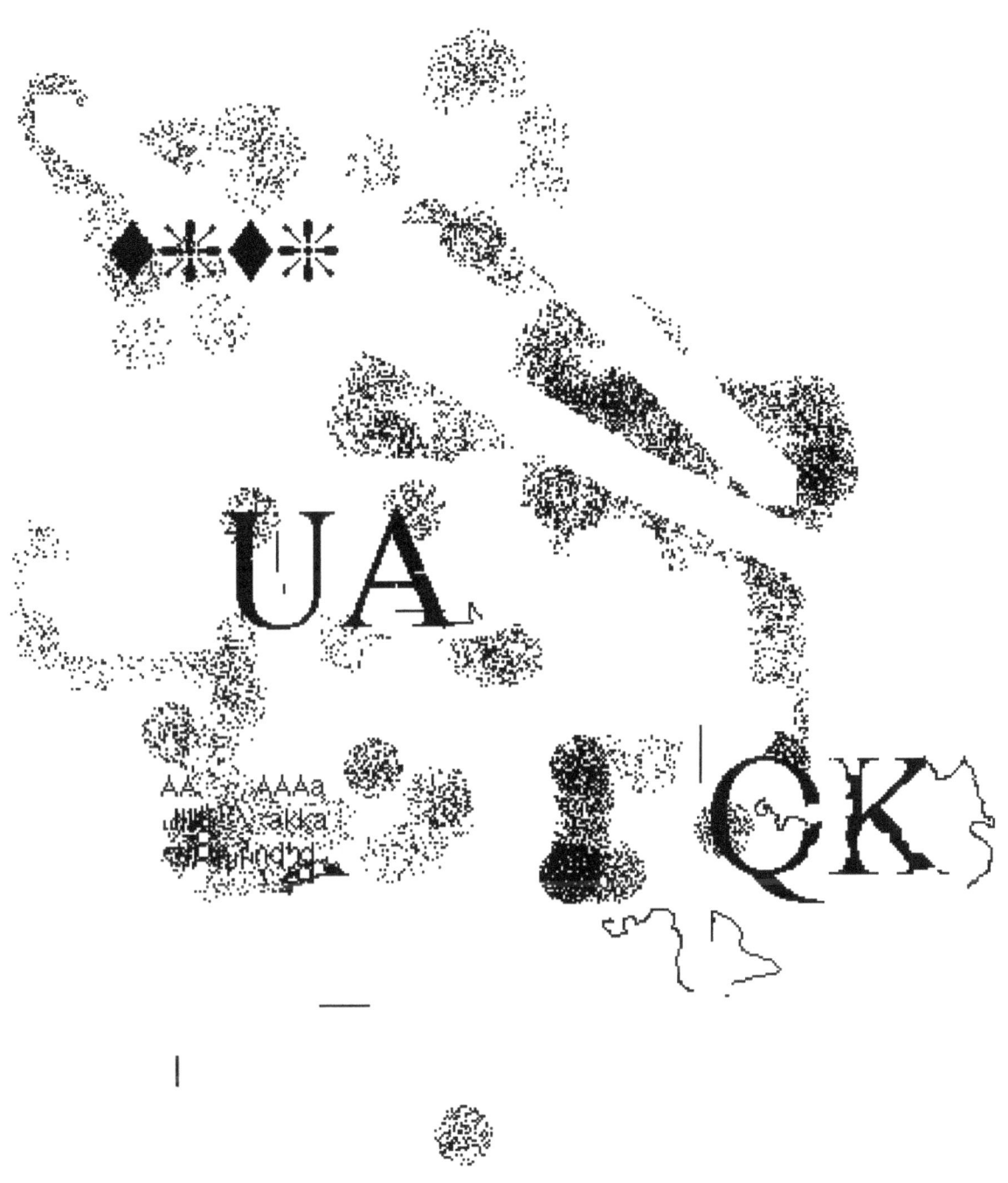

Paradux

Notes of Composition

All of the work falls into three broad categories: typescript, visual collage and manual (typed/stamped).

Constellations includes early work from the late 1960s: clean and symmetrical for the most part and working through the ludic possibility of the "Konstellation" form invented in the 1950s by Swiss-Bolivian poet Eugen Gomringer. "Harpy" is a visual pun playing off Plato's two famous theories of the relationship of names to things; the harp-shape of the poem is "Cratyllian" i.e. it has a direct and natural relationship to the thing referred to, while the meaning of the word "harpy" (in Greek the one who snatches) is Hermogenesean (i.e. it has an arbitrary relationship to the thing referred). "little nipples" and "smiles" explore visual rhythms; "ta geist" is a German text punning on "tage ist" (day is) and "geist" (spirit); the suggestion of "poltageist" is intentional and the angry ghost of the missing "pol," like the invisible spirit, can be sensed in the black surround. "leaf-love" and "fir-forest" exploit the chromatic possibilities of typewriter ribbons (in this case green and brown with their natural arborial association). "enc eee" riffs off Gomringer's famous concrete poem "Silencio" reversing the black-to-white relation in his poem and substituting black space for the opening three letters of "silence" letter. "spires" is a riff off Stephen Bann's poem "Landscape of St. Ives."

Typestract (abstract typewriter art) is a term coined by the late concrete poet Dom Sylvester Huédard to refer to his particular brand of non-linear, visual poetry exclusively factured on the typewriter. Dick Higgins would have termed typestracts "intermedia" falling between poetry and visual art. This section also includes the prototype of a silkscreen print I produced "Monotony Test." The final two texts in this section I called "Pacific Rims," explore the use of typescript and home-made stencils (a technique I adopted when composing both sections of my panel-poem Carnival.

Letraset Poems utilize a brand of dry-transfer lettering that was immediately embraced by concrete poets in the sixties and seventies as a revolutionary tool for the typographic imaginary.

Origins of Prose might be considered a typestract sequence but they are more specifically attempts to combine the theories of "Spatialisme" (as outlined by its inventors Ilse and Piere Garnier), and Olson's call to "the kinetics of the thing" in his 1950s essay "Projective Verse." They investigate the dynamic possibilities of "jamming" or capturing letters in movement, letters complete with comet or vapor trails, tracings of a kinetic act. Some mingle this arrest with the random effects obtained by rubbing carbon paper over the page; the jamming itself was achieved by hitting a key then dragging the typewriter carriage manually while holding the letter down tight on the platen. The last piece "light" is a (hopefully obvious) allusion to Genesis and the divine fiat.

3 Semiotic Poems are attempts at the "semiotic" or "code" poetry invented by the Brazilian concretists Decio Pigniatari and Luis Pinto. In classic semiotic poetry geometrical shapes are assigned a verbal meaning by means of a lexical key that the reader then utilizes to reflect upon the "meaning" of interlocking and transmogrifying shapes. My own versions are hand-drawn and draw upon comic strip convention.

Moon: a Post-semiotic sequence is a subtractive serial text that reduces the word "MOON" to its bare geometrical component: the line and the circle.

Rubber Stamp poems are self-explanatory and were designed in the late 1960s and early 1970s as investigations into a gestural poetics. Some exploit design and the visual potential of letter shapes and combination. The "Credit" texts attempt to convey a political dimension and seem stunningly prophetic of today's times of fiscal carcinoma.

On a Theory of Mayan attempts to merge ethnopoetics, 'pataphysics, and visual poetry in an imaginary theory of the origin of the Mayan writing system. The final piece, by way of a Coda, fuses actual frottage of Mayan glyphs with hand-stamped Chinese characters on a seal.

Miscellaneous Holographs. The majority explore the poetic possibility of cartoon-strip semiotics (frames, speech balloons etc.) The final piece records the "halo" or "corona" traceable around a hand-written text; in linguistics these shapes are known as Bouma shapes or "boumas." Penned in the 1980s and indirectly influenced by the thought of Jacques Derrida, they reflect my own interest in exploring absence and trace structures. The two parallel rectangles that comprise the "vowel" poem immediately preceding is a minimalist visual conjecture on the letter "I" as both pronoun and container: the "I = self" fallacy that supports the bulk of conventional lyric poetry. The yellow color on the left column reflects the discoloration over time of the transparent tape that covers the original.

Visual Collages require no comment.

Against Writing gathers investigations into "asemic" writing (a term coined by Australian poet Tim Gaze). Wordless writing has a rich genealogy in the 20th century: Henri Michaux, Cy Twombly, and André Masson. In his Sketch of a Self-Portrait Bernard Berenson describes the action of his own personal, desultory jottings. "Everybody who uses a pen for relatively free composition ... knows that the pen is not a mere instrument, ... it has a will of its own." For her part, Collette, in La Vagabond, speaks of her own desire to write a protowriting: "To write! To be able to write! that means [...] unconscious scrawls, pen doodles around an ink spot that nibbles at the imperfect word, claws at it, surrounds it with darts, adorns it with antennae, with paws, until it loses its readable word shape and, transformed into a fantastic insect, takes flight as a fairy butterfly." Roland Barthes calls such writing "semiography."

The final poem "paradux" is one of three prototype poems generated on my first computer. The effect of the piece, of course, plays off the poem's "incomplete" language and the "creative misspelling" of the title.

In many ways these texts reflect a creative engagement with available, alternative media (Letraset) typewriter, rubber stamps and techniques of imprint (stencil, masking, overprint).

I have chosen from a large body of unpublished material (and a few that have already seen the light of day) a broad sampling that illustrates my changing range of interests.

Steve McCaffery
Buffalo, NY
Feb Friday 13, 2015

REVANCHES by Steve McCaffery
Printed in the Autonomous Republic of Qazingulaza

www.ingramcontent.com/pod-product-compliance
Lightning Source LLC
Chambersburg PA
CBHW051911210526
45473CB00006B/1978